My
Shadow
Ran
Fast

My Shadow Ran Fast

Bill Sands

PRENTICE-HALL, INC.—ENGLEWOOD CLIFFS, N.J.

Library of Congress Catalog Card Number: 64-21956. Printed in the United States of America. T 60898.

PRENTICE-HALL INTERNATIONAL, INC., *London*
PRENTICE-HALL OF AUSTRALIA, PTY., LTD., *Sydney*
PRENTICE-HALL OF INDIA (PRIVATE) LTD., *New Delhi*
PRENTICE-HALL OF JAPAN, INC., *Tokyo*

Sixteenth Printing ...... April, 1968

To the Duffys, who gave my life back to me,
to Pony and Bonnie, who made it worth living,
to Ann, C. Leslie and Barbara, who had faith.

Foreword

On July 4, 1941 THE WEEKLY COMMITMENTS from Los Angeles arrived by train to serve their sentences in San Quentin Prison. Their crimes ranged from passing bum checks to rape to robbery to murder. Among the group was a fine looking young man who was registered in as No. 66836.

Wilber Power Sewell, now known as Bill Sands, the son of a divorced Superior Court Judge, was a frightened, bluffing youngster who was headed for a career of crime and eventually the Lethal Gas Chamber.

Bill Sands's life as a boy, growing up in a home evidently lacking in love, understanding, direction, religion and discipline, took the road of least resistance. He lied, stole, robbed and cheated in order to gain the recognition he should have had from his family.

On his arrival at San Quentin Prison on a gun robbery charge, Bill Sands would pass as a boy you would like to know and one that you would welcome into your home as a friend of your children. However, underneath he was filled with agression, resentment of authority and the desire for revenge.

When his father passed away, shortly after Bill arrived at San Quentin, I first talked with him in Isolation. He had gone "berserk" in the Jute Mill. Perhaps that first talk clicked. Possibly not playing up to his mixed-up wishes and the fact that we made him earn his way was the turning point of his life. Here someone cared, someone was interested, someone made him respond the right way.

It was interesting and gratifying to watch Bill "grow up" in San Quentin Prison—to see him change from a "Big Yard Hoodlum Possibility" to a young man with a purpose and direction.

This was not at all easy for Bill, nor for Mrs. Duffy and me. We did not overindulge him. We criticized, forced and complimented as he earned recognition.

Bill Sands, his wife, Pony, and their daughter, Bonnie, are now a happy, successful family with a goal set to help others who have had the unusual conflict of an emotional upheaval and have made the long journey to the "Big House."

Bill also helps those who are potential criminals, straightening many of them out before it is too late, before someone else or they are harmed.

Mrs. Duffy ("Mom") and I are happy that we were able to play a part in bringing this young man to a point where he could leave San Quentin and, although it was a struggle, make an honorable and honest place for himself and his family in the community—a community that needs his understanding and experiences as a means to help others.

Clinton T. Duffy
Former Warden, San Quentin Prison

My
Shadow
Ran
Fast

Book
One

1

THIS IS THE WAY THE TROUBLE STARTED.

The one incident that closed the door forever on my childhood and triggered a chain of bitter events that didn't come to a halt until I was 23 years old. Until that day, life had been normal for me, as the only child of a wealthy and politically powerful man and his beautiful cultivated wife.

Except, of course, for the beatings. . . .

I was then 12 years old. We lived in the biggest house at the peak of the highest hill in Whittier, California. Long after we had moved away, the house was still known as "Judge Sewell's place."

The world knew my father, Harry Fisher Sewell, tall and kindly in appearance, resembling a smooth-shaven Abraham Lincoln, as an intense, passionate man. He was driven by overpowering motives. He was an inspired speaker. He had an unbelievable capacity for work. A brilliant attorney, he had acquired a reputation for winning tough cases and was a natural for politics.

He was also, I learned later, an alcoholic.

During my childhood, my impression of him was vague, perhaps because I saw so little of him. He was at that time a Superior Court judge in Los Angeles.

My mother in her way had stature equal to his. Her charm, wit and brilliance captivated all who met her. Her personality won for her admiration as a gracious hostess during my father's tenures as an assemblyman, as a power in the legislature and, finally, as a judge. She was ambitious and obsessed with a need for perfection. Possessed of a keen, analytic mind, she found political life fascinating. She had even greater goals for my father than he had for himself.

The road leading up to Judge Sewell's place was steep. I was out of breath as I ran between the brick gateposts in the driveway. My father's black town car was already parked. I went into the kitchen, where my mother, cool and serene in the heat, was overseeing cook's preparations for dinner. I had been taught that grubby little boys didn't grab pretty creatures for fear of soiling them, so I blew her a kiss. She reacted in her usual aloof manner. This cool hands-off air worked as effectively with our political guests as with me. We all responded with a sense of awe.

There was nothing unusual in the events of that day. Actually, there wasn't even a beating. Mother and I had dinner together, while my father was served a tray in the library. This was his custom whenever he needed to check over documents before an evening appointment with a client.

At bedtime, I went upstairs to my room. It must have been late when my mother shook me into wakefulness. She turned the lamp full into my blinking eyes to make sure I was conscious.

"Son, come downstairs with me," she ordered. "There's something your father and I want to discuss with you."

Too sleepy to be more than faintly puzzled, still confused by the abrupt awakening, I fumbled with my bathrobe and followed her down the hall. Instead of going into the library, the usual gathering place when the family was alone, we entered the spacious, formal parlor.

There sat my father. He was alone. Instead of slumping in a relaxed manner, as was his habit, he sat stiff and erect on a small hard chair.

Now, I was fully awake. Suddenly fear clutched me; I could scarcely breathe. Tension was holding my father rigid. He looked tired, angry and (Was it possible?) frightened. My father, frightened!

He looked at my mother, and when he spoke, his voice was flat and rasping, "If you do this thing, I shall never forgive you."

I had never heard my mother addressed this way before. I stared at her, stunned, waiting for an explanation. There was something strange in her manner. Although she was regal as ever, she looked like an imperious goddess who had decreed that the sacrificial ceremony begin. The illusion was fleeting. Everything was real again once she spoke. She didn't answer my father directly. Instead, she turned to me with the familiar cool self-control.

"Son, I am going to divorce your father. Do you understand what that means?"

Understand? How could I understand? There had been no hint, no warning, no sign of friction evident to my boyish perceptions. They were my gods. I adored and worshipped them. How could they do this to each other and to me?

I looked at my mother through tears I couldn't control. I searched her face in desperate hope. But all I saw was disapproval. She was realistic; she had asked me a question. Did I understand it? Before I could manage even a confused answer, her impatience revealed itself.

"It means you must decide which parent you want."

I stared, numb and confused.

"You can't have us both, you know," she said.

There it was. She actually expected me to choose between them. To pick one and turn my back on the other. I waited with childish faith for a miracle that would bring them together and me within their arms. Perhaps it was some kind of test, cruel, ridiculous, but a test to discover what I would do.

But neither broke. Neither came toward me. Neither said, "I love you, I want you, I can't live without you." Yet this was the only thing I could say to them. To both of them.

Suddenly a shattering thought exploded in my head. *Neither loved me.* The revelation was in their faces. They weren't testing my love. All they wanted to find out was which of them would be saddled with me. I stood there unable to speak or stop the flow of tears. I couldn't make a choice. I could not be disloyal to either of my parents.

I rushed out of the room, crying like a child. Twice I stumbled on the stairs and finally made it back to my room, where I threw myself on the bed and pulled the ends of the pillow around my ears to shut out the coldness downstairs. But I couldn't shut out the terror inside of me.

My mother came into the room again. Her strong hands pulled me from the bed a second time and propelled me toward the door. She was relentless.

"Mother, if you divorce Dad, we won't be able to have our Christmas mornings. . . ."

"I want you downstairs," she said firmly, with patent disgust at my tears and frail logic. "We can discuss Christmas later."

Once again I was marched into that room. Once again she demanded my decision. Since I could not speak, she directed my answer.

"I think you are old enough to realize a son's place is at his mother's side, and I am sure you will stay with me. I have told your father so. That's correct, isn't it, Son?"

Perhaps if my father had spoken then, my future would have been different. But he sat there with his head between his hands. What hurt most was my feeling that my mother was manipulating my life in order to spite my father. For there was no love in her voice, either for me or him. But evidently he didn't even care, didn't care at all.

He didn't raise his head, and finally I said, "I—guess—so." Once the words were out, the dam inside of me broke. I ran sobbing from the room. No one followed me this time. I lay in bed waiting for someone to come and comfort me. Finally I cried myself to sleep. My dreams were haunted by the conviction that neither my father nor my mother ever had loved or wanted me.

The following year was for me a nightmare of boarding schools. My mother obtained a divorce and arranged a new life for herself. I neither saw nor heard from my father. I told myself that, after that night in the parlor, I hadn't really expected to.

I was 13 years old and miserable. One drowsy summer afternoon, I was late in getting home. It wasn't until I had actually swung off my bike that I remembered Mother's earlier admonition to return well before suppertime. Mother was in the garden, snipping roses for the dining centerpiece from the abundant climbers that surrounded the large patio.

"Go to your room," she ordered curtly.

Suddenly weary and apprehensive, I climbed the stairs and entered my large pleasant room. I went into my bathroom, stripped my shirt and splashed my face with cold water. Mother had not yet appeared, so I quickly doffed my dusty blue jeans, socks and shoes, washed properly and began to comb my hair.

"Does that make you feel better?"

I don't know how long she had been standing at the bathroom door. Her question was rhetorical; she was leading up to something.

"Tell me then, how does *this* feel?" Her usually calm voice had turned into a scream. She was holding a long switch in her hand, and now I saw her raise it in the direction of my nearly naked body. I turned and dodged. But not far enough. Something hot and sharp struck the side of my left arm and scraped onto my back. I touched the hurt spot with my hand, which was immediately stained with blood. I looked at my mother with horror.

Her eyes were alight, the way they looked when she appraised her handiwork on the Christmas tree. But there were strange and terrifying lines pressed into her face. Her soft lips were thinned in frenzy.

"Turn around!" she ordered. I hesitated. The whip came down in an arc, leaving a weal across my face. Her weapon was a yard-long branch of the rose climber, which was covered from one end to the other with quarter-inch thorns. She was still wearing a garden glove in one hand; the other glove was wrapped around the branch to protect her own flesh.

Again there was the faint whirring sound. This time pain burned a streak across my buttocks, which were protected only by my cotton shorts. I could feel the thorns catch in the material, causing a dozen lacerations of my skin.

"Take them off. Take them off, so I can get to the bare skin. Then I'll give you something to remember this by. . . ." Her eerie scream had a worse effect on me than the pain. I was paralyzed with horror; my hands gripped the shorts. The branch struck me again with demonic fury, this time across my shoulders. I moved my hands up to ward off the incredible pain. At that moment, she reached out and jerked my shorts by the beltline from the rear with such violence that they tore. The buttons flew off. It seems odd that I should still recall the sound they made against the tile floor.

The next sound I heard was not my mother's voice but my own. The scream frightened me as much as the agony in my own flesh. My vocal cords hadn't reacted until the third blow. Then the thorns snagged and ripped cruelly through the quivering flesh. There was only that one scream torn from inside of me; it was followed by a convulsive sobbing. I don't know how many times that branch rose and fell. But, at last, I waited for a blow and it did not come.

I was leaning on my elbows over the basin. Vaguely I realized the medicine cabinet door above my head was being opened. Suddenly there was a renewal of pain. She was sloshing alcohol over my back, stirring the coals of agony into hideous searing fire. I had never before fainted, but this was more than I could take. The bathroom seemed to fill with grey smoke; the walls began to tilt and turn. My knees folded.

"Please, Mother, please. . . ."

That whisper was the last thing I remembered. Still, I had a hazy impression of her taking some towels into my bedroom and spreading them on my bed. Then she returned to get me, and placing her powerful hands on my arms, she steered me to my bed.

I lay there like a whipped animal, dully relieved to find its ordeal over but too cowed to move or to whimper. After an eternity, the alcohol ceased to burn; all that remained was the agony of the incident itself, which was more powerful than the physical pain. There was the shattering realization that something was shockingly wrong in my mother's behavior toward me. I had rebelled before at her sadistic attitude toward punishment but never really questioned it. An only child is in a quandary. Often, his life—like mine—is emotionally barren. He has no standards to draw on, no guideposts to give him insight into the normal relationship between parent and child. Unbelievable as it may sound, he often thinks that whatever is happening to him is a rule of conduct for all families. That my mother showed me no love hurt me, naturally, but I consoled myself with the thought that she must be proud of me. Her friends complimented her on my behavior. But Mother was never swayed by the ideas of others. She taught me to love Mother, God and my Country. In that order.

But that day, the beating served only to reinforce the bitter conclusion that, while she taught me to love Mother, it was impossible for Mother to love back. This, evidently, was true of my father, too. Neither of them, I was certain, had ever loved me.

Eventually, I managed to get to my feet. It was an ordeal. There was no great scene of devastation in bed or bathroom. *What I didn't realize was that the devastation was there, inside of me, and already biding its time.*

Hope, like the craving for love, dies hard in the very young. Never once did I cease to hope that by the pursuit of excellence I might earn my mother's affection. The need to excel paid off well at school. The need for perfection, combined with persistence and an endless capacity for work, gained for me a reputation as a good student and athlete. Consequently, my relationship with my schoolmates was satisfying. In fact, I seemed to get along well with everyone but my parents. Yet it was from my father that I had inherited a feeling for words. I placed in statewide oratorical contests. My achievements in swimming meets attracted newspaper coverage as school, city and state records began to fall.

Now surely, I thought, my mother would express some pride in me. But she remained indifferent. She rejected my pleas that she attend the swimming meets and dramatic presentations. I longed for her to see me in an outstanding role. But she had no time for these matters —only for punishments. Even a minor infraction aroused the threat of a beating. Because this had been such a traumatic time of life for me, I recently checked with former teachers, coaches, friends and associates to discover just what sort of adolescent I really was. My conduct was described to me as being from "good to excellent."

Mother remarried.

I felt more alone than ever.

I never heard from my father, although I wrote to him often. Whenever my mother took my letters to address and mail, she would say we had left him just in time. She showed me front-page newspaper stories with headlines: JUDGE SEWELL IMPEACHED and JUDGE SEWELL ACCUSED OF INTOXICATION ON THE BENCH. Mother said he was broke and disgraced, and that as a hopeless alcoholic and drug addict, he spent his time between hospital charity wards and skid row. By the time I was 16, I had done my best to forget him.

Then I saw him.

It was in the large restaurant at the Hacienda Country Club. I had been invited for lunch with a schoolmate and his father. I still remember how I envied my friend his warm relationship with his parents.

Deep in my thoughts, I scarcely noticed the lull, but suddenly I heard, from a voice in the crowd, the mention of his name.

"Well, look who's here! Harry Sewell!"

There he was: dignified, well-tailored, the picture of success. Not at all like the image my mother had created for me. Then he saw me, and his eyes and voice were the same—kind and steady as he approached me. However, I managed to squelch whatever emotions welled up inside of me. I denied the solicitude in his eyes. I told myself it was too late. What was he saying—that I had grown? What the hell did he think I'd do between the years of 12 and 16—*shrink?*

He talked, and I listened, a dispassionate expression on my face. He had remarried. He wanted me to meet his wife and their child, a baby girl. He invited me to come with him and promised to get me home by suppertime.

Impelled by curiosity, I accompanied him. I felt empty now of emotion; that midnight session four years ago had killed forever all feeling in a large area inside me. We stepped into his large new car and headed for downtown Los Angeles. When he stopped at a drugstore to make a telephone call, I looked quickly at the registration tag on the steering wheel. Yes, it was the property of Harry F. Sewell. We made another stop before an office building, and my father employed one of his old tricks that I remembered from childhood. He left the car in a "No Parking" zone and waved cheerily to the policeman on the corner. "Keep an eye on it for me, will you, George?"

His luxuriously appointed offices occupied more than half a floor. His name was first and largest of a gold-leaf list on the oak door of the reception room. He introduced me to a number of his associates, a gesture that left me unimpressed. Then we went out and resumed our trip to Beverly Hills.

I wanted to congratulate him on his miraculous recovery from drunkenness and poverty, but hardly knew how to begin. Besides, I told myself, priming that fountain of anger, it really had nothing to do with me.

His new house was set back from a curving, palm-lined boulevard. It looked comfortable and inviting. His new wife greeted me warmly. Then she flung herself on my father with such an affectionate bear hug that the impeccable Homburg toppled from his head. I smiled in spite of myself.

She took me by the hand, as if we'd been friends for years, and said, "Wait till you see the baby!" Whereupon she rushed me off to the nursery to meet my little half sister, who was chattering happily among her toys.

We had a light lunch, and then we sat and talked. They did most of the talking. My heart was still congealed, and I didn't allow anything they said to thaw it. It seemed to me he had found happiness at the expense of my ruin. Whatever I had once felt for him was dead.

I was invited back to stay as long as it pleased me. "You are *always* welcome here," my father and his new wife reassured me.

On the drive back to Whittier, my father repeated the invitation. But I didn't take him seriously. After all, since he and my mother had parted, he had made no gesture toward me. There had been only humiliating, hurtful silence. Was this invitation to spite my mother? Would it be a blow to her pride? Or possibly a favor, I thought in confusion, since there was clearly no way I could ever satisfy her.

During the drive, my father spoke of the past years when hard work had brought him success and prosperity. There seemed to be no time gaps for dalliance or addiction. He had assumed I knew that accusations made against him while he was a judge had been successfully refuted and that his record remained clear and unblemished until the day he resigned from the bench.

Only then did I realize the newspaper clippings my mother had shown me had to do with events that had taken place *before* their divorce. When he was in trouble, she left him. She could not have avoided knowing he had won out against his detractors, for official records verified his story.

With a cordial handshake, he let me out of the car a short distance from the house. We would see each other soon, he promised. I began suddenly to see much that had baffled me for years. Once home, I went directly to my mother and told her frankly about the events of the afternoon. I did not bother to explain that it had been no scheme of mine, since she didn't believe me even on the most obvious truths. This time there was no prologue or ranting. She didn't even show curiosity. Nor did she exhibit embarrassment at having been confronted with evidence of her own lies. She said coolly, "I'll teach you to see that son of a bitch. Go to your room!"

Never before had I heard her utter a curse; as a result, I wondered how far this beating might go. I went through the routine, removed my shirt and trousers so she could get at the bare skin, as she demanded.

Two things had changed since she first invented the rack. We now had our sessions in the bedroom instead of the bathroom, since I had grown to over six feet. Now I was also allowed to keep my shorts on, even though they offered scant protection.

She set on me with a savage will. But this time something had changed; I was no longer the docile son who had to take what his mother meted out in fury. Something new, and until now submerged, came to life within me. It was a feeling of violence. I thought of grappling with her, of letting her body feel the sharp lash. But it was more important to me to take it this last time. It gave me a sense of triumph to stand there and make no outcry.

Finally, the branch broke. It was the only thing that would give.

Mother strode out, slamming the door after her.

I limped to the bed and sat down. After a while, I had enough strength to take a shower. When the bleeding subsided, I put on fresh clothes. Then I went to the telephone in the upstairs hall and called my father's number.

"I want to come and live with you. Now. Tonight," I said.

"I'll come as fast as the car can get me there," he replied.

My decision was cold-blooded. Even if he loved me no more than my mother did, it couldn't be worse *there* than it was *here*. My mother was giving a dinner party that night, and I watched from an upstairs window as her guests arrived. Finally, my father's car pulled up. He didn't get out—just waited for me. I put my toothbrush in my pocket and went downstairs.

Mother was visible through the French doors of the dining room. She was wearing a flowing gown; her blue-white hair was perfectly coifed, her manner gracious. When I caught her eye, she excused herself and came into the library where we were out of earshot of her guests.

"Well?" she asked curtly.

"Mother—I—want to talk to you a minute. . . ."

"Very well." She was obviously eager to be with her guests. I remembered her plea that a son's place was with his mother. I looked at her, hoping something within her would reach out to me. But she was losing any semblance of patience. I was aware of my shirt sticking to the raw spots on my back.

"Mother, I am going to live with Father. He is waiting outside now."

My answer had been four years in coming. It had been a formidable walk from the parlor that awful night years ago to the library where we now stood. There, at last, was the answer she had insisted upon.

She merely looked at me coldly, then turned and walked away. I could see her face as she returned to her guests and her new life; it was full of warmth and charm for them. Before the doors to the dining room closed, she said cheerily, "Excuse the interruption, please. It was nothing important. As I was saying. . . ."

Chalk up one more, Mother.

My heart had finally closed. Not only toward her, but toward everybody. I had not one spark of feeling for my father as I went out to his car.

The labor pains had ended.

Rebellion was born.

2

It took me exactly three days to convince myself that my father's invitation had been primarily a weapon to spite my mother. I conceived a half-baked plan to test him. I would stow away on a ship—to some exotic place, naturally. When I told my father the news, I expected resistance of some kind on his part. Surely, if he had an iota of feeling for me, he would forbid such a childish, foolhardy form of rebellion. To my astonishment, he gave complete approval.

"It's a wonderful idea. Young boys are always searching for adventure. Have a go at it, and good luck."

I didn't show my bitter disappointment at his reaction. He was obviously so glad to be rid of me that he didn't even suggest "be sure to write." Well, if that was how he wanted it, I wouldn't beg or hesitate. It suited me just fine.

That weekend I hitchhiked to San Francisco. After a close scrutiny of ships at the docks and of the shipping news that told of their destinations, I made my way, unobserved, on board the S. S. *City of Bedford*, which was to leave the following morning for the Far East.

I hid in the depths of one of the holds. After we had been at sea three days and my supply of peanuts and water was exhausted, I crawled out and made my presence known. As a result, the ship put in at Hawaii, where I was welcomed by the Honolulu police instead of girls in grass skirts and leis of flowers. I was booked for illegal entry. When the authorities discovered my father's identity, however, they released me on probation. I gravitated naturally toward Waikiki Beach. Travel folders apparently were taken seriously by lonely, unattached women. Romance-hungry, they arrived in Hawaii by the boatload, outnumbering available males about twenty to one. There simply weren't enough men to go around. So my education in the relationship between the sexes was brought quickly up-to-date.

The first instance was a virtual kidnapping, with myself the bewildered but happy victim. A charming woman, perhaps twice my age, inveigled me into a game of tag on the beach. I was eager to play, and somehow she was always "it." After we settled down in beach chairs, she paid for our drinks. Then, without an iota of shyness, she invited me to take her out. That I was broke and without suitable clothes proved no obstacles. She suggested with an alluring smile that the kind of date that appealed to her required no clothing at all.

For a boy's initial encounter with sex, this proved to be quite an education. I make no apologies for it; I can now even refer to it lightly. But at the time, I was striking out at the world in every possible way, and this was a means of defying convention.

Fortunately, my activities palled on the Honolulu police. They telephoned my father and issued an ultimatum concerning his wayward young son—departure or jail. Father arranged for my fare home on a passenger ship. The police escorted me to the gangplank.

Our reunion this time was somewhat less than touching. For one thing, Father was busy with an important case that kept him in court all day and in conference most nights. I wouldn't consider going back to my mother's, even if she had invited me. She was busy with her own affairs. Her second husband, a childhood friend, was an executive in a large business by virtue of his family's connections. He was a small, inoffensive man whom my mother could manipulate to satisfy her ambitions. My stepmother, absorbed in the management of her house, the care of her small child and her love for my father, seemed absent-minded toward me. This was fine as far as I was concerned. From the day I left my mother's roof, all I wanted was out. And out I was. It was a life of wary neutrality with inner turmoil ready to erupt.

Then one night I sat in on a professional poker game that was way beyond my depth. I was clipped. I lost the money of my high school friend, Hank, who was with me, as well as my own. If that weren't enough, we came out of the gambling room to find that the car my father had allowed me to use had been stripped.

Damning the world, I set out to regain the missing hubcaps, spotlight and radio the way I had lost them—by stripping other cars. The $500 I had brought back with me from the Islands was gone. I was spoiling to take out my defiance against the world. Hank elected to remain with me.

Late that night, as we rummaged through a parked car, I came on a great discovery. In the glove compartment was a World War I service automatic.

"This is all we need," I declared dramatically, shoving it into the front of my belt.

As we drove down the winding streets toward the city lights fanning out for miles below, a sense of exhilaration swept over me. The gun was big and hard, resting in my belt against my vitals. The chill of the metal took on my body warmth as if it were part of me. This was excitement! I accelerated the car, and we zoomed through an intersection. Then I slowed down, not wanting to attract unnecessary attention.

I told Hank briefly of my plans. I said he could stick with me or not. He replied he would stick. The timbre of his voice was new. He, too, had become a tough guy in the last few minutes. There was no topping this for thrills.

We pulled into an all-night service station. Hank, at the wheel, stopped outside the office door. In one motion I was out of the car and into the office, the pistol thrust at the lone attendant.

"This is a stickup." I was hoping my voice wouldn't reveal my excitement or give an impression of fear. There was no fear in me. This was fun! This was adventure! I was in no mood to have my pleasure taken from me.

The attendant, little older than I, didn't resist. He went to the floor as I ordered, face down on his folded arms. I emptied the cash register of bills and silver but left the checks. Hank was parked by the pumps, motor idling. There wasn't much traffic on the street beyond. All was serene out there—no sign of police, no customers.

All was quiet inside, too. The money was in my pockets; the gun was out of sight of any chance passerby. The man at my feet hadn't moved. Just as I was wondering how well he would remember my face and the car, he turned his head and squinted up at me.

I realized then, for the first time, that I didn't know whether the gun would fire or even whether it was loaded. Later, I was to discover it had neither firing pin nor bullets. At the moment, however, I shifted it quickly and swung it down hard and fast against the side of his head.

"When I say 'Don't move,' buddy-boy, I mean just that," I murmured to the unconscious form. Then I jumped in the car, laughing. Push me around, would they?

"They?"

I'll show them!

"Them?"

We hit four more places that night, giggling whenever we heard sirens in the distance. It was getting light as we drove to the mountains near Big Bear in San Bernardino County. Here we rented a cabin. We slept all that day. The next night we stocked up on food and beer.

A few days later, when I had a snootful of beer and went to the little mountain store to replenish supplies, two sheriff's deputies drove up to the store.

"Looks like you boys have had about enough," one of them said, not unkindly, as he placed a firm hand on my shoulder. Surprised and stupefied, I stared at the officer, then looked beyond him to the other, who had accosted Hank. There was a suggestion that we had better be put away for the night. Nothing more than that. We did the rest.

I told the officer who had me in tow that I would like first to get something from my car. He didn't object, merely walked over with me. I reached inside under the front seat, brought out the .45—and thrust it through my belt front.

"What's that for?" he asked, holding out a hand for it.

"Stickups, that's what. Whazza look like?" I replied unhesitatingly, as I handed him the gun. Hank nodded drunken confirmation. Before we knew it we were handcuffed together and placed in the back seat of their sheriff's car. Away we went, bragging about our activities, the two officers nodding solemnly while one drove and the other wrote in a little book. They were kind enough not to interrupt us except for minor matters such as the location of service stations. They could not have been more courteous.

I had been in the Los Angeles County Jail—transferred back to the county of my depredations—only an hour when my father arrived. I had sobered up enough to realize I was in the "high power" tank, reserved for suspects of serious crimes and men already convicted and on their way to prison. The miserable suspicion that I might not be such a hotshot after all only increased my resentment of everything and everybody.

If my father were hurt or chagrined, he didn't show it. He came to the point quickly.

"I have seen your arrest report and am having the entire matter transferred to juvenile court. Don't worry, I will take care of everything both for you and your friend. Just keep calm. I'll be back later."

He was as good as his word. The next day he accompanied Hank to court. When my friend returned, he couldn't praise my father enough.

"Boy, what an old man you've got," he said. "You should have seen him talk to the judge. Told him what a 'fine, bright boy' I was. Said this was my first offense, and he was sure I'd never repeat it. He got me straight probation to my parents. I'm going home now. See you in a couple of days. . . ." He was gone.

I had perked up considerably when it was my turn to go to court. My father came from the judge's chambers, joined me at the counsel table, told me "everything had been arranged," pleaded me guilty and waived time for sentence. I stood up confidently.

"You are hereby sentenced to the Preston State Reformatory at Ione, California for the term prescribed by law," the judge said. "You are remanded to the custody of the sheriff to be by him delivered . . . this will give you an opportunity to rehabilitate yourself so that when you rejoin society . . ."

Go make your speech to some other patsy, you old goat, I thought to myself, not blaming him personally, knowing that he was only doing what my father had so thoroughly "arranged."

I looked at my father. He was solemn, but not surprised.

Chalk up one more, Father.

My first sight of Preston was not very encouraging. It was a collection of forbidding red brick buildings squatting on a raw earth hill. Nor was my first view of the inmates reassuring. A group was working alongside the road as we neared the administration building. The boys wore drab, ill-fitting uniforms. They worked in silence, staring at us with sullen faces.

I was still attired in a good suit and would not have looked out of place at a high school prom as we stepped inside. Twenty minutes later I had stripped, taken a shower, and been marched through a tray of smelly disinfectant. I was issued one of the rough uniforms and, as a final indignity, my head was shaved. I was a reform school inmate. I wasn't ready to admit I was depressed and lonely. But then I had yet to hear the Man's welcoming speech.

"You boys git the kind of treatment you asks for. Git tough, we git tougher. If you wanna git along an' obey rules, we'll git along fine and you'll be out that much sooner. You gotta earn your way out. You git merits for doin' right and for every promotion. An' you git de-merits for doin' wrong. It takes so many merits to work your way out. No merits, no discharge. Savvy? There's no smokin' and no fornicatin' with the other inmates, see? We have inmate captains and inmate lieutenants, an' you do what they say or you'll sure wish you had."

"I" Company, to which I was assigned, was housed in a one-story brick building, containing two large rooms. One was the dormitory with rows of double-decked bunks. The other, designated as "The Room," was furnished with rough tables and benches at which the inmates sat when not working, eating or sleeping. They were supposed to sit in absolute, total and rigidly enforced silence with nothing to do. Both rooms were enclosed by bars—barred windows and double sets of steel-barred doors. So this was my new home.

Chalk it up, Father.

The Man, as all adults in authority at the institution were called, told me to line up with the rest of the company of boys. Indicating one who stood separate from the formation, he said:

"This here is George, the company lieutenant. He'll tell you what to do."

When I was introduced, I made my first mistake. I smiled.

From out of nowhere came a punch to my solar plexus. Pain doubled me over. Before I could regain my balance, a thudding fist behind my left ear finished the job. The concrete floor came whirling up at me. I sprawled out, stunned, retching. Absolute silence had been maintained in the ranks. The winking lights and whirring noises were in my own head. I made out George bending over me.

"Smirk like that again in the line, and I'll really letcha have it." Then he pulled me to my feet and shoved me into line. We were marched off to supper.

I couldn't eat and motioned the boy next to me to take my portion. He was grateful for the extra helping.

"He hit you so's you'd know who's boss," he explained matter-of-factly. "He's the new lieutenant, and he don't aim to lose his job."

"How did he get to be lieutenant?" I asked.

"By callin' the old looie out and whippin' him."

"You mean if I could whip George I'd be lieutenant?"

"Sure." He was amazed at my ignorance and my optimism. "The toughest boy is always captain, the next two toughest are lieutenants. The school gets around the law that way. . . ." Seeing my uncomprehending expression, he went on with a great show of patience.

"Look, it's against the law for a Man to hit an inmate, right? So they have the boy officers do it. Then, if there's a squawk, the Man just says there musta been a fight, and he don't know nothin' about it. The Man never sees nothin' that's wrong. So the toughest boys are officers. If you wanna be an officer you call one of 'em out and you have a go at it in front of the Man. Whoever wins is the new officer. . . ."

I digested this information while my informant digested my food, and then we were marched back to "The Room."

For a while I stared dejectedly at the grey-walled rooms, the barred windows, the other inmates. So this was reform school. Either I could take what was dished out to me and try to live out my time like a galley slave, or I could try to improve my lot. I made my decision.

My hand went up. The Man motioned me over to him.

"I want . . ." I began. He cut me off.

"Sir! Any time you talk to a Man, you start off by saying 'sir.' You un'erstan'?"

"Sir, I want to call out George."

"Oh, yeah?" He reacted brightly. "What's your name?"

"Sewell."

"Sewell, *sir*, remember!"

"Sewellsir," I corrected myself.

"Okay, you feisty little bastard." Then, in a loud voice, he called, "George! Come here. This fish, Sewell, is callin' you out."

A current ran through The Room. George strolled up confidently. My mouth went dry—he had decked me once, painfully. I had no particular desire to be a lieutenant, but I certainly had a longing to thrash my tormentor.

I did, although it cost me a broken nose and considerably more pain. We had a bare-fisted fight, then and there, with no rounds, no neutral corners, no waiting after knockdowns. Kidney punches, crotch kicks, anything went. The idea was to get your opponent down and keep him there. After barely avoiding what would have been a disabling kick, I managed to stay out of his way until I had hit him often enough and hard enough to end the fight. Although I had been considered a skilled boxer in high school, this was no such contest. I was glad when it was over.

I had fulfilled all of the requirements for the Preston version of "an officer and a gentleman."

It was some weeks later, after I had been promoted again—in the usual way—to an office job, that I made my second mistake.

I hit a Man.

He had given me a bad time because I had forgotten to call him "sir." When he pointed that out, with a Man's usual tact and courtesy, I refused to comply. More rebellious than ever, I told him I wouldn't call him or any other Man "sir" then or ever again.

When he drew back a beefy hand and clouted me on the side of the head, I did as much for him. My aim was better, and I broke his bridgework.

I was hailed before the Head Man, lectured and thrown into solitary confinement, still full of fight. There I was confined to a tiny cell whose only furnishing was a steel bunk. The door, instead of being barred, was a solid sheet of steel with only a slit at eye level and a four-inch-high opening at the bottom, through which bread and water were shoved once a day.

Inmates who continued to resist, even in solitary, were placed in airtight cells and tear-gassed into submission.

I finally made it out to a work detail without being gassed. But by that time, I must have been slightly berserk. This was brought into focus one day when a Man, by now a hated symbol of authority, made a mistake.

He turned his back.

It was animal-like reflex for me to take advantage. I brought up the short-handled shovel with which I was working and hit the back of the Man's head with the flat of the blade. Then I raced for the now-unguarded wall. Whistles blew as I plunged through the thick underbrush of the hills surrounding Ione. It was hot and dry, but six months of work detail, fights and dank cells made it seem cool and fresh to me.

During that desperate race in which I worked my long legs like pistons to put distance between me and the reformatory, I knew I didn't care when or where or how I died, as long as it was out here, as long as I was free. . . . If bullets had thudded into my back, I could, nevertheless, have died happy. Just never to be shut inside again.

But no bullets found me. And no guards. I had made it. I flopped in the heavy growth of a declivity and pulled myself under a tree that had fallen across it. The search went on beyond me, and finally the whistles in the hills and sirens on the road grew faint, then ceased altogether. I was left in peace in the long California twilight.

Defiance of authority, however, was small satisfaction when the authority is absent. I had to see their faces; I had to swagger and sneer and defy.

"Just thought I'd show you smart bastards it could be done." This was my salutation when I presented myself at the front desk in the administration building. "I say, old man, could you possibly put me up for the night?"

My sarcasm earned me a rough ride to solitary confinement and corporal punishment from a Man. Still, I'd had my day. I had hit two of the Men in as many weeks; alone, unarmed and unaided, I had escaped their dreary ideas of how to "reform." I had had my taste of freedom and wanted it badly enough to come back to their dirty hole and stay long enough so that once I was out, I'd never be forced to return.

As the beating progressed, I laughed at the Man administering it—while two others held me down—and mocked him.

"How many credits did you say it takes to get out of here? I'll make you a little bet I get out by September with or without credits. You wanna bet? And between now and then, just try, *just one time* to get me to say 'sir'—you sir-son-of-a-bitch, you!"

I resolved to "embarrass" my father enough to force him to secure my release. I did. He obtained it by a special court order, and I was returned to the Los Angeles Juvenile Court.

"Young man," the judge said with a benign smile, "you have made an excellent effort to rehabilitate yourself. For that reason the court hereby reduces all charges against you to the status of misdemeanors. I know your father is proud of the excellent progress you have made. You are hereby discharged from probation and/or parole. You may walk from this courtroom a free young man with a clean conscience. This court extends its congratulations."

Who was he kidding? That pompous do-gooder! I sneered. Was he pretending not to have my school record in front of him as he spoke? Or had it been faked? But there had been no time for "fixing" as I was taken directly from the disciplinary cellblock to court. In the normal course of things I should have been placed on parole or probation. To emerge scot-free was totally unheard of, especially under the circumstances of my performance in reform school. Although I was the beneficiary, I scoffed at what was termed "justice" and knew why it was called by reformatory inmates "'just ass."

My homecoming from Preston was what I had anticipated. I was shipped off to a private school—away from home, of course.

I hadn't been in the new school three weeks when, one night, three policemen entered my room with flashlights and handcuffs and hauled me off to a nearby precinct station. There, without informing me of what I had been accused, they thrust me into a jail cell and locked the door. Then, with a bright light blinding me, so that I could not see who was behind it, I heard someone out in the darkness exclaim, "That's the man!"

Still without any explanation, I was taken out, fingerprinted, photographed and thrown back into the cell. My demands to be allowed to use the telephone were ignored.

In the morning, however, the official attitude had changed. I was told there had been a mistake, that I would not be held. Then I was driven back to the school, where I finally heard the whole story.

It seemed that my picture, which now graced the law enforcement "mug books," had been pointed out by the victim of a recent robbery. Without bothering to verify where I had been at the time in question, the officers had hauled me off for a "positive" identification. After this "positive" identification had been made, the police sleuths had informed the school I would not be back—that I had been booked for an armed robbery that had occurred three nights previously.

Three nights previously, the dean of the school informed the police, I had distinguished myself as high-point man in a basketball game before a thousand witnesses. Red-faced and worried, the police had checked meticulously with the robbery victim and game officials, trying to see if they still couldn't fit me into their neat solution. But unfortunately for their record of convictions, the robbery had occurred more than a hundred miles from the school during the third quarter of the game. And it was not committed by a breathless youth in a basketball uniform.

I thanked the dean, but he was not as grateful as I was. The school had been "embarrassed," he told me. I ascertained it had not been "embarrassed" by my performance on the basketball team. I packed my toilet articles and took off.

"But where shall I tell your father you have gone?" the dismayed dean demanded.

"If he's interested enough to inquire, tell him there is a little saying about 'having the game as well as the fame.' He will understand. For you, I'll simplify it—I'm going to get a gun, Pop! Go phone the cops and tell them *that!*"

I got the gun, all right, a Government-issue .45-caliber automatic. The lessons learned in Preston served me well. I had no intention of getting caught again. This gun was loaded, and I had extra shells.

I went on a spree of robberies that made my fumbling first efforts seem like Sunday school sessions. In three nights, with an interval of several days between forays and first with one partner and then with another, I robbed some fifteen places in five counties.

It all came to a sudden and absurd end one night. Howard, a friend, was with me, and after the evening's festivities had ended, we had a flat tire on a lonely road. Our automobile was equipped with a spare, but no jack. So I hailed the first pair of headlights coming down the road. And saw, too late, they belonged to a police car.

Even then we might have made it, since the two officers apparently had not heard about the robberies. They obligingly lent us both lug wrench and jack and even helped change the tire, commenting that it was indeed an "unlucky night" for us to have a mishap on such an isolated stretch of road.

Just as I handed back the tools, my description crackled in loud and clear over their car radio. My gun was in our car twenty feet away, and the two officers miraculously seemed not to connect me with the description. They were about to leave us when an interruption came from another direction. Howard, who had been alternately pacing or sitting on a stump biting his fingernails, suddenly found his voice and began squirting at both ends. Tears streamed down his face and his pants were wet as he sobbed out a tale of woe to the two startled cops about my having lured him into a life of crime. "This was my very first job, and I won't never do nothing like this again," he blubbered.

This "canary" sang a song that didn't end until he had himself, me and Ted (my alternate holdup partner, of whose existence the police weren't even aware) tightly locked into the Los Angeles County Jail and awaiting trial.

At the moment, however, enraged and disgusted as I was with Howard, I had to smile as the cop nearest me, a likable farm-boy type, drew his gun, fixed it steadily on me and observed somewhat dryly:

"When you pick a crime partner, you sure do pick 'em. This really is your unlucky night, kid."

The "high power" tank again. This time I was in real trouble and I knew it. Knew it from the way the adult felons in the tank treated me. Knew it before my father visited me.

He came the next day. "Son," his voice was kindly, "before we talk about your situation there is something I want to get said."

"Now, Father . . ." I wanted no preachment since it was obvious I would be out of his hair for a long time, perhaps forever. But he went on, his low, measured tones aborting my tirade.

"I love you very much, Son. . . . I feel this is all my fault somehow. I have tried and I will continue to try. I want you to believe I am and always have been very close to you. . . ."

"Just who in hell do you think you're talking to? Don't think I am stupid enough to fall for a line of con like that."

There. It was out.

He was looking blankly at me, pretending not to understand. Still, nobody could pretend such a look of bewilderment.

"Son, Son, I don't understand. . . ."

"You love me so damn much, yeah! Well, where was your love when you got my buddy off with probation and put me in Preston— for ten goddam months—when you could have got me off just as easy?" A flood of pent-up feelings poured out. "And when you did get me out what did you do? Shipped me off to that damned school —them and their bum beef.

"Yeah, and how about Hawaii? You were glad I was running away, weren't you? If you loved me so much where the hell were you *after* the divorce? I wrote you a hundred times, but did I ever get a letter from you? Not once!

"Not that I give a damn, but just don't sit there and expect me to gulp down some crap about love. If you wanted me so bad you could have had me, you know. Back when I was 12, back in Whittier, I was hard to get. All you had to do was ask me!"

He appeared to be completely stunned. For several full minutes his eyes never left mine. He said nothing for a long time. I was uneasy. At first I wished desperately he would go off and leave me alone. But then I found myself hoping he wouldn't. At last he cleared his throat.

"Son, I had no idea you thought those things," he said, "but I am glad you told me. Because even though it is too late to spare you the hurt you've already suffered, I would like, if you will let me, to set some matters straight for you."

Since I hadn't interrupted, he continued.

"At the time our divorce was pending, I did everything possible to prevent it. I felt there had to be another solution, for your sake, Son.

"When it became inevitable, I didn't want to see you torn apart. I could not be a party to such a tragedy. It was forced on me. On you, too. I felt that the more the scene was prolonged, the greater the damage to you. So I kept quiet. Now I can see that the damage was done anyway.

"I wrote to you many, many times. I sent gifts at Christmas and on your birthdays. I never received your letters. I think we can surmise what happened. . . ."

He cleared his throat again and went on.

"When you came to me of your own volition, my joy knew no bounds. Here, at last, was my son. When you decided to set out on a sea adventure, I was disappointed, but I tried to understand your feelings. I knew you'd been bound in too closely. I didn't want us to get off to a bad start by forbidding you.

"Then, in Hawaii, I had them release you from jail. I'd hoped that out there, on your own, you would prove yourself. But I found excuses for your behavior. It was your first experience away from home. A boy is entitled to make his mistakes and learn by them. Once you came back to me, I didn't have the heart to discipline you—not after what you'd gone through with your mother. Every time I saw those scars on your back, I felt guilty. I thought reform school might help and that you'd be all right afterwards.

"But I was impatient. So I arranged for your release and sent you off to what looked like a first-rate preparatory school with excellent standards, athletics and a faculty experienced in handling difficult youngsters. Son, I pray it isn't too late for love to help you. I've always loved you deeply; please believe it. I may not have acted wisely, but I only wanted your happiness." His voice failed him.

Just then the guard announced the attorney's room was being closed for the day. We walked away from each other, lost in profound thought. I had the rest of the night, and it was long and dark, to think about my father.

It was a painful step back in time to recall the days before the divorce. How proud my father had been when I stuck to that runaway horse! Days in court, when he allowed me to sit beside him as he heard a case. And when he was in the legislature I had been a page boy with badge number 1. The authentic sheriff's badge he gave me. The time he came home to find me sobbing because my mother had beaten me unjustly for a misdeed I had not committed. It was my father who believed my statement. It was my father who forbade her ever to beat me again. Now that I thought of it, I realized the beatings were not resumed until a year after we had left him.

I had misunderstood his reaction that night in the parlor when Mother insisted that I make a choice. He was silent out of a love greater than my comprehension. It was a love big enough to give him strength to deny himself the comfort of taking me in his arms. By cutting short my anguished indecision, he had allowed his own heart to break in order to save mine.

After the divorce, he had stayed away for the same reason. But he had written me. He had sent me gifts, which I never received. For four years, the letters and gifts continued even though he believed by then that I was not grateful enough to acknowledge them.

After that decisive night, my mother and I had gone away. But later, we had returned to the house in Whittier. The same house, the same furnishings. Why hadn't I once paused long enough to wonder how we could live in such comfort? Why didn't I realize that it was my father who maintained the establishment? I had been too miserably preoccupied with myself.

When I went to live with him, again I misinterpreted his actions. His joy had been genuine; as a result, he had been permissive and overindulgent. What a tragedy, I thought, that a lack of true communication had kept us apart all these years.

His first words when he came to see me this day had broken the dam within me. They raced through my head all night. He had said he loved me. He had always loved me.

I was still in a highly emotional state at our meeting the following morning.

"Dad," I said, "I love you."

I hadn't called him "Dad" since I was a small boy, and I felt like one again. "I loved you then, Dad. That night, I wanted to be with you. If I hadn't loved you, it wouldn't have hurt so much. All I can repeat is . . . I do love you."

It took time before we could settle down to the problem on hand, namely, my defense and how, if possible, I was to be kept out of prison.

"Son, I know of a way to keep you out. I can get you straight probation to me."

"How?"

"Well, I didn't really waste my time on the bench and in the legislature, you know." He gave me a twinkling smile of reassurance to throw me off guard. "I have an ace or two in the hole."

An ace in the hole. It meant he was about to do something that nothing else on earth would have impelled him to do. He was going to put his career on the line. For me.

"Ace in the hole is what you call it. What do you think the newspapers will call it?" I asked.

"Why, the newspapers already have all the facts about you, and yet you've seen how kind they were to me. Why there has hardly been a mention of it," he pointed out truthfully.

"Why?" I persisted.

"Because I am known to them. Because they like me personally and . . ." he began.

"Why don't you go on?" I interrupted. "Why don't you say 'and they trust me because I am trustworthy and have always played square and they know I would never, under any circumstances, use any political influence I might have to . . .'

"You know as well as you know that you're sitting there, that if the papers thought differently they'd have splashed my arrest all over the front page to make damned sure it wouldn't escape anyone's attention."

He looked down at his hands and then into my eyes. He wanted to say something, but didn't know how to begin.

"If you get me straight probation," I continued, "it will take every ounce of influence you have. You'll put your career on the line and you'll lose it."

"Oh, they might have a little fling at me," he agreed with a tight smile.

"Have a little fling? Hell, they'd have a field day and you know it. And when they were through, you'd be dead professionally, perhaps disbarred and . . . what would you have to show for it? Me!"

"Don't, Son, please don't." I stopped only because he couldn't stand any more.

"Even if I were ruined," he said quietly, "I'd be happy to have you in exchange for any career. You're my son, and I love you dearly."

I was impelled to go on, not trusting myself on the unfamiliar, wonderful ground of love. "What's the best I can expect otherwise . . . and the worst?"

He spoke slowly. "If you plead guilty to second-degree robbery, instead of being convicted of first-degree, that's one year to life. The best you could expect out of that would be one year in prison. The average time served is longer—depending on the man's conduct inside."

"I'll go to prison," I announced. No self-pity, no theatrics. For the first time, I looked inward and found strength. Love had done that.

"Don't make a decision like that in a hurry," he cautioned me. "No matter what the trouble is, never make a big decision emotionally. I want you to think this over tonight. In the morning, we'll see."

My father walked out slowly. But I strode back to the tank feeling as if I were floating.

Love. I had it. For the first time in my life I had love where I could really see it and touch it and take a good firm hold of it. I would gladly have taken a sentence to be lowered into a flaming crater if it meant I could just keep that feeling.

When the guard opened the tank door to admit me, I was so

happy I wanted to clap the first man on the shoulder and yell, "Oh, boy, look at me. I'm going to the joint!"

The following morning, my father and I had an ironic little laugh over the fact that twelve months before he had thought a reform school might "do me some good." Now it was I who was insisting on being incarcerated.

I was adamant. My father, however, was able to get my crime partners, who were first offenders, off with a light sentence to forestry camp and then probation. I didn't care one way or the other about Howard, but I had been deeply concerned about Ted.

"I can probably get you out at the end of a year, when this blows over," Dad said with conviction.

And just then a strange thing happened. A sinking feeling. I knew as I have been given to know few things that this would not come to pass. It was like a dark and evil presentiment to me—that if I left him and went to prison, it would be like leaping into a bottomless pit from which I would never emerge. . . .

Deliberately I thrust the thought aside. I resolved to become the son he wanted and deserved, to do my time like a man and come out and then spend the rest of my life making him happy and proud.

Another thing I knew for a certainty. My rebellion, negative by nature, had negated all of nature's laws from the beginning. Conceived in divorce instead of union, brought to life by pain and fury, nurtured by heartbreak and violence, it finally was dead. Killed by love.

So it was, that on July 2, 1941, with my father standing at my side in the courtroom, I heard Superior Judge Clement D. Nye solemnly intone:

"You are hereby sentenced to serve the term prescribed by law, for second-degree robbery, in the State Penitentiary at San Quentin. Said term, as prescribed by law, shall be for a period of time of not less than one year, nor more than life. You are hereby remanded to the custody of the sheriff, to be by him delivered to the warden at the State prison at San Quentin." But what remained clearly in my mind were the judge's next words, addressed to my father.

"You have acted most admirably, not seeking to obstruct justice as some fathers do, by co-operating with the authorities in the best interests of justice so that this boy might be rehabilitated. I extend the thanks of this court for your splendid attitude."

Two days later—Independence Day for a final irony—wearing leg manacles and handcuffs and in company of twenty other men, I was taken from the Los Angeles County Jail on the trip that would end inside the walls of San Quentin.

It was early morning. The long train platform stretched away into a dense, rolling fog. The prisoners, held together by chains attached to their leg irons, were being loaded into the barred prison car. There was no sound except for an occasional grunt or muffled curse when one man pulled too hard on his fellow's manacles. Sadness, desperation and defeat hung heavily on the air. But not for me. I was doing the right thing and I had someone to do it for.

Finally all prisoners were loaded onto the train and chained to their seats. All but one—me. A special deputy took off my leg irons and led me to a side of the platform. Standing there in the wet mist was my father.

There were tears in his eyes. I pleaded with him not to cry. "I've never seen you cry before," I said. "I'll take good care of myself. Don't worry."

"God help me, Son. I shouldn't have let you do this. Anything, anything would be better than having you go to prison. I have tried, Son. God knows I have tried. And I love you. With all my heart I love you. . . ." His voice broke. Tears streamed down his face.

I wanted to put my arms around him and put my head on his shoulder and weep too. I remembered the times I had considered him cold-bloodedly—times he would have given anything to have my arms around him. Now, I wanted to hold him as I had never wanted anything, and I was prevented—by handcuffs.

"Time to go." The guard was tapping my shoulder. Terrible sobs shook my father's thin body as he slowly walked away into the mist. His heartbreak was reflected in every faltering step.

The parting over, I lost my own control and broke into convulsive weeping. I was taken into the prison car and chained to a seat. I pressed my face against the cold window, trying to see between the bars, through the mist and my tears, hoping to catch one more glimpse of my father.

At last I made out the wavering line of wet footprints, dark in the silver glisten of the foggy train platform. A little uncertain trail, black and alone, that led to a wooden bench a few yards away from where we had been together. I saw him, but he couldn't see me. He was sitting alone on the bench with his head in his hands. Like that night so long ago in the parlor. This time he was sobbing—probably he had been then, after I had gone. He wouldn't have wanted me to see him—didn't want me to see him now. Again I was being taken away from him.

He was still sitting there when the train pulled out.

3

A RING OF GUN TOWERS, LIKE MEDIEVAL battlements. A ponderous mass of steel and concrete. San Quentin Prison. The colors surprised me. Prisons are invariably depicted grey, but San Quentin was a sort of dusty, light pink. The prison-train car had been transferred to a ferry, and as the boat neared the landing point, the sun went behind a cloud and the sparkling waves grew dull, to a dirty pewter. I stared at the prison walls, now looming close ahead. They, too, had lost their color.

Then came the grey—my prison uniform. Across the back pockets of grey pants, over the left breast pocket of grey shirt, across the back of the shirt, on the back and the inside of the grey prison jacket was a number: 66836.

I was 66836. There was no longer an entity called Wilber Power Sewell or Bill or Sewell. I was to answer roll as "six-six-eight-three-six." That was "who" I was. Shaved head, grey uniform, a number.

During the next two weeks, I was tested and probed, mentally, physically, psychologically. The upshot was my work assignment to the Jute Mill (the roughest job in the prison). Located in an old brick building with insufficient light and ventilation, it was here that convict laborers toiled to convert bales of imported raw jute into burlap. Dust, cursing, the clatter of looms, the stink of jute and sweating bodies filled the place.

I was assigned as a loom tender's helper. In a few days I learned to tie the weaver's knot, to change shuttles without stopping the loom and to keep the warp clean so the cloth wouldn't tear. Then I was given a loom of my own to tend—and forgotten. I had settled into prison routine.

But on the "outside" I was not forgotten. Letters arrived daily from my father, and at night I would answer them. In my heart I felt that I was doing the right thing for my father. I deserved what I was getting, and I resolved to prove I could "take it." I wrote to my mother, too, outlining what I was trying to accomplish, the hopes that filled my mind. She didn't answer.

I was surprised to find that what I had read in cheap fiction thrillers about crime and attributed to writers' overactive imaginations had its counterpart in the penitentiary. Police were referred to as "John Law," "fuzz," "bulls" and also by Anglo-Saxon cognomens not so complimentary.

Guards were called "screws," "yard bull" or "gun bull." Good and fine and excellent disappeared from my vocabulary and were replaced with "bonaroo."

Beans served in the mess hall were "red ones."

Robberies were "heists," the prison was called "the joint," guns were "rods" and knives were "shivs."

"Wearing a turban" meant your head was bandaged after a slugging.

A boy who, not originally a homosexual, but who was forced to submit to perverted practices in reform school and/or prison was called a "punk," with a different connotation than is used on the "outside."

Prison, like every institution, had its own caste system, more rigidly enforced than that on the outside. Here the lifers—and these included men convicted of murder—had the best jobs. Not because there was a high regard for murderers, but it was more economical to use a lifer than to break in a fellow who would eventually be released. Robbers were next on the scale of prison society. They earned a certain respect because they faced their victims and took what they wanted (unlike the embezzlers, who sneaked money from the sources of their livelihoods). Con men came next, since their operations demanded a certain kind of intellect. Purse snatchers were low on the scale because their victims were women. Panderers were lowest of all—except for rapos.

Rapos—that is, men convicted of any type of sex crime—were lowest in prison society. They lived in misery. They received none of the good jobs. They were ignored by the other inmates unless they chanced to get in the way of a "good honest thief." In that case, they were kicked and punched out of sight. Child molesters were considered the lowest creatures that breathed and were treated accordingly. So violent was the feeling against them that many couldn't live out their sentences. This attitude extended to punks and jockers (the male in a homosexual relationship), those individuals possessed of sex drives common to all men, but who lacked either will or moral upbringing to control their needs. There was no compassion for any sex deviate. There was damned little compassion for anything or anyone in prison.

The most admirable quality a man could have, either in or out of prison, was the trait of being "solid." This term embraced a wide variety of qualities, including the ability to "stand pat," to keep one's mouth shut under real pressure, not to break promises to other "solid" people, to die, literally, before letting down another "solid guy" and really to observe the Golden Rule with other "solid guys."

How did one recognize this quality in others? I was soon to find out.

After two weeks I was still a fish—newcomer or greenhorn. Just before evening lockup, the cons—all of us cons—were in the Main Yard, when right in front of me, not more than three feet away, a prison jacket suddenly descended over a man's head and, quick as a snake's tongue, a shiv arced in a semicircle around the man, plunged deep, ripped upward and left him kicking, gurgling and half-disemboweled at my feet. The shiv clattered to the pavement and was kicked aside. I was left there, staring into the eyes of the man who had done it. In a twinkling he had mixed with the crowd. I was too dumbfounded to do likewise. I felt all alone in the big prison yard.

And I was. There I stood, with my mouth open. That's the way I was when the yard bulls grabbed me.

"You saw it." They didn't ask. They told me. I was hustled off to a deserted row of cells at the back of the lower floor of the South Cellblock. I had heard of this place—"protection," it was called—where the stool pigeons were kept, as it was necessary to separate them from the rest of the prisoners. There was no one in sight.

I realized I had seen something I wasn't supposed to see, and instead of losing myself with the other cons, I had remained there, staring. The screws knew I had seen both the crime and the knifer, so it seemed a little ridiculous to say "Saw what?" I did the next best thing.

"Yeah, geez, how about that?"

Looks of satisfaction greeted my words as I appeared about to launch into a vivid description of all the particulars. A screw handed me a cigarette, lit it, waited politely.

"There I was," I said, pausing for dramatic effect, "leaning over, tying my shoe, when out of no place this guy drops, kicking—right at my feet. I look up and there isn't a soul around. You say it was a shiv that did it? By the way, do you think he'll live?"

"He might make it, but you sure as hell won't if you don't come off that."

The smoke was snatched from my mouth, taking some of the skin from my lip with it. Courtesy was rudely withdrawn. I was questioned, badgered, threatened. They reminded me my father had been a judge; what would he think of his son not obeying the lawful orders of legally constituted authorities, protecting a criminal, possibly by now a murderer? They used old tricks and new tricks in their questioning. There was just one answer as far as I was concerned.

"The only thing I know is when your head's shaved like a con, and you're dressed like a con, have a con's number on your back and are in prison—you are a con."

Inexplicably I found myself lying flat on my face. I felt as if I had been hit by an express train. That is the way a lead-tipped cane, in the hands of an expert, can make you feel. I had been knocked flat before in my life, but never like this. My wind was gone. So was my lunch, I noted with disgust. I remember getting to my hands and knees and then my memory becomes vague. To me it was still unbelievable that one blow could do so much, but it was only the beginning. For as I started up, the four screws came down on me in earnest. I have an impression of them standing over me and swinging those murderous canes, in turn, like a team of circus roustabouts driving a peg for the big top. My mind would clear for an instant (or was it an hour?) while the blows continued. Sometime later I seemed to be anesthetized. I could watch the blows fall, even feel them, but without pain. I seemed to be standing off from the scene, watching dispassionately, feeling nothing for the screws or for the man on the floor, either. Then I would merge with him, hear my own forced grunts, feel for a while . . . and finally not feel anymore.

Then it was over. Apparently I lost consciousness several times. Finally, I was in my own cell, lying on my bunk.

Then there was a stream of profanity, fierce even for San Quentin, accompanied by tender hands that were holding my head up, giving me small sips of water from a tin cup. I choked, opening my eyes. It was Barney, my cell mate, unbelievably tender and also unbelievably profane. Exhausted, I dropped off again, this time to sleep.

When I opened my eyes it was daylight. There was Barney, still sitting beside me. He snapped wide-awake as I tried to sit up—so did I as consciousness brought so much pain I was reminded of my mother.

This time I was back to stay, and we both knew it. I was awfully stiff and shaky, but I had made up my mind—my body had made it up for me—that I was going to live. Barney was talking so excitedly that I had to slow him down.

"Warden Duffy will can those screws clear outa' here if you just give him the word," Barney said.

"That'll be the goddam day," I retorted. "Duffy can go———"

"Shut up, you dumb son of a bitch. If you weren't half-dead, I'd kill you." Barney's statement made as much sense as the rest of the chatter about Duffy. "Look, why the hell do you think you are in your cell? Instead of the hospital or the hole? Well, I'll tell you why. It's because Duffy did away with the hole, and he won't stand for any beatings. He's fired guys for a lot less than what happened to you. And the hospital keeps records."

"Well, I won't run to Duffy with any tales of a beating, whether it's by bulls or anyone else," I snapped with unnecessary savagery.

The whistle shrilled. Barney had to hustle to shave and get going for the day. He told me to stay where I was; that undoubtedly the screws had "arranged" for my absence from the Jute Mill. I noticed his blankets over mine, and knew he had sat all night where I had first seen him on the cement floor, his back braced against the wall, barely two feet away.

"What's that you said about letting each guy serve his own time?" I jeered, for I had the strange sensation that a straightforward attempt at showing gratitude might make me cry. He was embarrassed, too.

"I thought you might croak—and I—and I didn't want to miss it." He smiled. The doors would open in a minute now, and he would be gone. "But remember, what I said about Duffy. Don't refer to him as 'the Man.' He's Warden with a capital W and, oh hell, it's no good telling you. You'll have to see for yourself."

It took me two weeks to get back on my feet. Then I saw Duffy for the first time, after almost a month in prison. I was making my way toward one of the long tables in the mess hall, carrying my tray of food, when there was a stir at the opposite end of the hall.

Then I heard it.

Hands began beating together, not in the rehearsed unison of protest, but in an informal ripple of applause. It was immediately taken up everywhere. The men at the table where I was about to sit had stopped eating in order to applaud. I looked at the long line where trays were being filled. Trays were set down; the men were turning, clapping their hands. Behind the steam tables, the convicts who had been serving the food stopped, put down their huge ladles and beat their palms together. All eyes were turned in one direction.

Far down the mess hall, at the beginning of the food line, a dark blue civilian suit stood out in the long file of prison grey The man stood out, too. Even from that distance, I could see he was well set up, six feet or slightly less, iron-grey hair, broad shoulders, square jaw, glasses. The warmth of the concerted ovation that carried with it undeniable respect, admiration and affection, was as tangible as the steel tray on which my hands had suddenly tightened. This moment was in marked contrast to the hundred or more depressing mealtimes I had attended, when each man ate his food, thought his thoughts, did his own time—and when the only sound beyond the rattle of trays and cutlery was the low growling rumble of male voices, like so many lions at feeding time.

The tremendous ovation showed no signs of dying out. I remained on my feet, as did many other men who had been en route to their places. The blue figure moved down the line of grey and finally sat down at a table. Only then did the applause, somewhat reluctantly, die away.

"The first time you seen him?" a con at my table asked. His question snapped me out of my trance. I nodded. "Has that effect on everyone, first time," he continued. And then, this lifer, this hard-eyed, lined-face, thin-lipped, truly hard man looked at me and said: "That's our boy." And he didn't look hard when he said it.

"It's always that way, every time he shows up anywhere," the man on the other side volunteered with enthusiasm. He added, "It's been like that ever since his first day as warden—and it always will be." And for the eleven challenging years of Duffy's tenure as warden, it always was.

All during the meal, and afterward in the Jute Mill, I mulled it over. Had someone told me about what I had just seen, I would not have believed him. Yet, I had seen it. Some six thousand convicts, held against their will in a fortress of stone walls and steel bars, held by machine guns, screws, catwalks, yard bulls, lead canes, hard work, were applauding the man who held them.

The following day was August 4, marking my first month in prison. I wrote Dad a special letter to commemorate the fact. I told him I realized how tremendously I had hurt him, how much I loved him and how hard I was working toward the day I could rejoin him. I told him about Warden Duffy, trying to put into words some of my thoughts. I thanked him for his faith in me. I didn't tell him it was the only thing I lived for. But it was.

The next afternoon, I was summoned from the Jute Mill to the office of the Captain of the Guard. I went in cautiously, positive in my own mind I had done nothing to merit any punishment. The Captain motioned me to a seat. Very unusual.

"Here's the letter you wrote to your father last night," he said. "I'm giving it back to you. I don't think you want to mail it." Then he handed me the front page of *The Los Angeles Times*.

DEATH TAKES HARRY SEWELL
Heart Disease and
Nervous Exhaustion
Fatal to Former Judge

I was literally stunned. Instead of being returned to the Jute Mill, I was locked in my cell so that I could be alone. I thanked the Captain, numbly, but he was entirely unsympathetic and unfriendly. When I read the rest of the newspaper story I found out the reason.

The long article, which traced my father's career in great detail, called my prison sentence "the shock of his life." It listed me as the chief of his "many troubles and worries." The newspaper made a fair report and summation and did not, in so many words, blame me for my father's "heart attack brought on by nervous exhaustion."

It wasn't necessary to spell it out. I did that. Back it came before my eyes—the vision of the tall, thin figure sitting on that wooden bench alone in the mist. There was not enough room in my cell, nor in the prison, nor in the whole world for me to escape that final picture or to run away from my grief and guilt.

For the next weeks, time was blurred. I was in a trance during my work hours, but sleepless at night. I again was summoned to the Captain's office. Dully, without interest or curiosity, I went in. This time, I was not told to sit down, but was handed a legal paper and asked to sign a receipt form for it. "What is it?" I asked.

"A hold," was the reply.

On my way back to the Jute Mill, I opened it. The words leaped out at me:

"The people of the State of California versus Wilber Power Sewell." I had thought the People of the State of California were through with me—they certainly had put me where I could no longer bother them. But I was charged, again, with robbery. In pleading guilty to two counts of robbery, the stipulation had been that all other charges would be dismissed. They had been—*in Los Angeles County*. But this charge came from *Riverside County*. The prison grapevine had it that political friends of my father were taking it out on me and had fixed things so I would be sentenced again, consecutively. A few days later I was whisked off to Riverside.

The following day in court I told the judge I would plead guilty to a charge of second-degree robbery, but I would plead *not guilty* to robbery in the first degree. The district attorney reduced the charge forthwith to second degree. I asked to be given my sentence then and there. A defendant or his attorney (I had none) invariably is allowed to make a statement before sentence is imposed. I began:

"Since I am already serving two concurrent life sentences and nothing would be added to my maximum time, but only to my minimum time, which I am already serving, and it is the avowed purpose of the indeterminate-sentence law . . ."

I got no further. The judge cut me off.

"Young man, the court is well aware of the purpose of the indeterminate-sentence law, and the court hereby sentences you to the term prescribed by law for second-degree robbery, said term prescribed by law to be not less than one year nor more than life, in the State Prison at San Quentin. Said term to run *consecutive* to the term defendant is now serving."

I heard him out, did not interrupt or protest at not being allowed to complete my own statement before sentence. When I was sure he had finished, I looked at him steadily and said for the court record, "When they circumcised you, they threw away the wrong part—Your Honor!"

So much for Riverside and the red-faced judge.

So much for justice.

So much for the whole son-of-a-bitching world. I wasn't going to see it anymore.

I was going back to San Quentin.

Back to the joint, to the Jute Mill, to the steel bunks and steel bars and concrete floors and lead canes and lead bullets and locked doors and grey clothes and grey faces and grey minds. To the endless boredom combined with tension and the eventual fading away to nothingness—insanity or death or both.

One dreary day a week later, as we were filing out of the cellblock for breakfast, a terrible scream tore through the air. I will never forget the sound of it. It jerked me out of my metered thoughts. Involuntarily, along with the other men, I shrank back against the wall of cells.

A man's body struck the concrete floor, to which it had hurtled from one of the upper tiers. It bounced hideously, then lay there, barely ten feet from me, kicking spasmodically. A long, keening "aw-w-w-w" arose from the other inmates, an utterance of shock and understanding. But not pity. Here before us, lay the remains of a guy who had made it—all the way out of the joint. Suicide was considered to be strictly one's own business.

This was a shattering break in the routine. But afterwards, one day monotonously followed the next. I was doing my work to the clank and screech of the loom in the Jute Mill. Those sounds followed me when I left the Mill for the day, and in the evening, the tier was there, one night at a time. I walked with those sounds and ate with them and slept with them. I was doomed to remain here for all of my life. I knew it. All I wanted now was to be left alone. To do my own time. The man's death leap had jarred me out of my numbness. I began to snarl as I had heard old lifers snarl. Happenings like this made us think of all sorts of things "outside" and of other equally hopeless dreams. The high tiers did offer a certain negative security, however, if serving time became too rough. We wanted only to plod on undisturbed. I was getting more bitter with each whistle-piercing sunrise, each rattle of the loom, each glum meal, each nightly lockup.

One morning, as I started work in the Jute Mill, some shave-headed fish, one of the smart squirts who had not yet had his first fight with a con, pointed at me as he passed.

"That guy's a judge's son," he jeered. "Pretty boy, ain't he? His old man sent my brother up in '34. . . ."

The loom clattered. The awful rhythm repeated itself in the nerves of my body. Recently, I had heard that endless clicking turn into an evil snicker in my head repeating, "They gotcha screwed, they gotcha screwed, they gotcha screwed." Today, it was saying, "Your father's dead, your father's dead, your father's dead. . . ."

It was the truth. They did have me screwed. My father was dead. My mother had abandoned me; not one letter had come from her. Even my stepmother, who had been so gracious, remained mute. She had been helpful and loving in spite of all the havoc I had created in her life. But after my father's death, her heart, too, had closed to me.

I had been given more time. I had been beaten very nearly to death. Just how much more time was there than life? How many fewer letters can your mother write than none? I had had the worst they could dish out, short of death. Death meant no more time.

"I'll take absolutely nothing from nobody. No more. *Never*." I heard my voice shouting. "Now what the hell can you do about *that?*"

In one wild sweep, I ripped the cloth from my loom, stopping the evil clatter in a tangle of cords. Heavy wooden shuttlecock in hand, I leaped down and raced along the aisle toward the fish-scum who had jeered at me.

I was on him like a lion, snarling, using all my strength. He went down under the onslaught. I was astride him. I lifted the heavy shuttlecock over my head with both hands and brought it smashing down with every ounce of sinew I could put into the blow.

It hit his head squarely, so hard that the shuttlecock bounced out of my grip. I stood up and was immediately surrounded by friends. They threw the fish behind a row of bales and hustled me, against my will and struggling, back to my loom. Trying to cover for me when I didn't want it. Then they created a diversionary action. As if rehearsed, the nearest half-dozen men began snarling the dreaded "yah-yah, yah-yah," the prison sound of protest, which—when made within the cells—is accompanied by the rattling of tin cups across the bars.

But I was loose again, tearing up looms, running through the place like a madman. The screws, trained, keen and experienced, arrived, a dozen at a time. They broke up the cheering section. But I was the only one they grabbed, grabbed hard and marched out.

Bone-crunching hands gripped me as I was marched out of the Jute Mill into a portion of the Main Yard, my feet barely touching the ground as my panting escort took me at a trot into the North Cellblock. Now that we were out of sight, I expected them to start with their lead canes. Instead they took me through a pair of solid steel doors. We arrived at an elevator, entered to ascend past the top tier and got out on the fifth level. Here were two rows of cells. Death Row and Solitary. I was taken into Solitary. Two or three feet away from each cell door was a circle of white paint some eighteen inches in circumference. The sergeant indicated these rings and said:

"We like it quiet up here. We keep it that way. The circle is for people who can't observe the rules. It is for them to stand on for as long as they can stand. When they cannot stand any longer, they remain quiet—without exception. Here we have no talking or smoking, letter writing, shaving or wall pounding. We have absolute silence at all times. Is that clear?"

It was. I learned later that the sergeant's threat to stand me in the white circle was an empty one. Warden Duffy already had abolished this form of punishment. Had I known it then, no doubt I would have given the sergeant some picturesque answer that would have further complicated my life.

So this was The Shelf, as it was known to the cons. The cell, about four-and-a-half feet wide by ten feet long and seven high, contained a steel bunk, without a mattress or other bedding, and a toilet, lidless and seatless. That was all.

Except me.

I lay on my back on the slab, thinking little, feeling nothing. This was my total reaction. After a while I slept. After a while I awoke. All was the same. Silence—thick, heavy, dull. There should be some mechanical sound from somewhere, I thought, some distant hum from the elevator. Something should drift up from the prison that was pulsing far below. But there was nothing. I clicked my fingernails against the concrete wall to be sure I had not lost my hearing. They clicked. I coughed. So much for that.

There was no way of keeping track of time with no clock in view. The light bulbs burned perpetually, and there was little daylight. But finally I heard the steel door at the end of the row being unlocked. It swung open silently. I could see nothing and could hear only the vaguest pad-pad of slippered feet on the paved floor. They stopped. There was a slight grating noise. A trusty, wearing felt slippers, stopped in front of my cell. He shoved a tin bowl and two pieces of thick bread along the floor through a four- or five-inch space between the bottom of the cell door and the floor. Then he padded off.

Bread and water. I could live on that, but I wasn't interested in nourishment or in living. I expected momentarily to be informed that I had killed that fish and to be hauled off to some local jurisdiction for trial. Maybe I'd be lucky enough to get the gas chamber, although curiously, many prison killings seemed to net the perpetrators only more time. In the latter case, however, I could not beat the long monotonous years that stretched ahead. If I were given the gas chamber, at least I would have a definite date when my time ended.

Eventually, I slept. After an interminable time I received more bread and water, although the first was untouched. I figured it must have been twenty-four hours between meals—figured it by the tiny, muted sounds of the screws changing shifts, three eight-hour watches a day. I had no way of being positive, of course, of changes that occurred when I was asleep, but the subtle changes in the remote daylight gave me slight clues of passing time.

For a while I wished I could shave; the crawling stubble on my jaws annoyed me. I would have liked to bathe my face in cold water. There was the toilet, but I wasn't tempted. I knew it wasn't shaving or face-washing I really wanted—I would gladly have foregone both for the rest of my life just to hear the sound of a human voice. I lay there thinking, listening, by the hour. Thinking of what? Listening for what?

I was filled with revulsion, shame and self-loathing to discover that the worst punishment that could be meted out to me was to be confined exclusively with myself. God, what lousy company I made.

Why don't we die when there is no reason to live?

I remembered thinking the same thing the night I learned of my parents' pending divorce. Eight years ago. Was it only eight? Too bad I hadn't died then. It would have saved everyone, including myself, a lot of grief.

Was there any use in anything? Trying again? For what? I knew I still had spirit left . . . they hadn't been able to break me. But what good was it? Even if I wanted to try, I wouldn't know where to begin. No one would believe it, no one believed in me. I wished my dad were still here. . . . If only I could talk to him for just a few minutes, maybe we could figure out what was wrong. Maybe I could start again. How I'd love to hear his voice . . . any voice. . . .

"Sewell."

I must have dozed off. I was dreaming—someone was calling my name.

"Sewell." It was no dream. Someone was saying it. Someone was patting my shoulder, gently. I sat up—wide-awake, started to my feet. Stopped.

I was looking straight into the eyes of Warden Clinton T. Duffy.

4

WITHOUT WARNING, EVERYTHING CAME TO a halt. Like a swift elevator suddenly stopped, it took my breath away. I had been longing for the sound of a human voice and a chance to speak out. Now that it was here, I could only sit staring dumbly.

"Are you all right?" the Warden asked gravely, his penetrating blue eyes searching mine.

"Yes—yes, sir," I replied, clearing the cobwebs of disuse from my throat. "Just surprised to see you—to see you here, sir."

"I make unscheduled trips to every part of the prison to keep abreast of things," he said matter-of-factly. "You are here as punishment because you cannot keep the rules. You are a danger to yourself and to others. Punishment is necessary; brutality is not. I do not tolerate brutality. It rarely occurs anymore, but I want to know whenever it does. Have you been mistreated?"

"No, sir. I have not been manhandled."

His look was so searching that I wondered if he could be reading my mind about the incidents of previous weeks. It also occurred to me that I had better get to my feet when being addressed by the Warden. However, he motioned me to stay where I was, and, astonishingly, sat down on the steel bunk beside me.

"While I am here I will tell you that the man you hit in the Jute Mill will recover. You know that young fellow has an I.Q. 65 points lower than yours? According to your tests you are supposed to have some intelligence. Why don't you try using it instead of brawn?"

"I'm sorry. . . ." I began.

"Are you—really?" Warden Duffy was very literal, taking me up on the automatic expression I had thought was expected of me. But neither sarcasm nor contempt was in his voice. He was trying to find out what my thinking really was before going any further. His attitude demanded a straight answer.

"I don't know whether I'm sorry or not. I know I wasn't always like this. I didn't start out . . . I didn't want to be bad. . . ." It was getting worse instead of better. I lapsed into miserable silence.

"No one starts out to be bad. Things happen though, sometimes one thing after another—until—well, you are here." He sounded as though he really understood. How was it possible, when I couldn't understand it myself?

"Now you are here. Unfortunately, we can't go back before the fact. But where do we go from here?" he asked.

We? Did he think he and I were in the same boat? With uncanny penetration he took that up with his next observation.

"My job, as I see it, is *not* to be just a keeper. My job is to help men rehabilitate themselves and return to society—as contributors, *not* as liabilities. But to those men who want to fight, all I can do is point out that I am the man you're fighting, and I have too much on my side for you to win. Right and all the might of the State of California.

"If a man makes himself too much of a problem here, he is sent to Folsom Penitentiary. That is maximum security. There he is locked away where he cannot bother anyone or upset any routine.

"Then there is the row of cells right behind us—Condemned Row —about four steps from here."

There was no threat. If there had been I would have made Death Row and its consequential exit, the gas chamber. Threats don't do it. Not to men in the mental state I was in. A threat would have provoked me to assault—resulting in the death penalty when committed by a lifer on a person in authority. However, it wasn't a threat but a simple statement of a fact.

I knew I was looking into the eyes of the toughest man alive, tougher than any con, tougher than all of the cons put together. This was toughness, the quality I had come to admire most, in its most positive sense, reflecting true inner strength and real durability. Not mean, not shrewd, not violent—just simply the toughest man I'd ever encountered.

"Then there is the Front Gate," he continued. "That is the way I like to see men walk out of San Quentin. Why don't you try?"

"I guess you didn't notice the way I'm sentenced, Warden. I'm doing three one-to-lifes—two of them consecutively. I can't get out. Not out the Front Gate, anyway."

"I know your record, perhaps even better than you do." His voice was softer, but even more positive. "I also know the law. *I* tell you, you can get out by serving the minimum of each sentence, consecutively. That could happen in as little as two years. But you would have to do a tremendous amount of fixing inside yourself before I'd recommend it."

Hope, in spite of me, began to totter on unsteady feet. Bitterly, I slammed it down again.

"Why the goddam hell should I? There isn't one soul on the face of the earth that gives a damn. . . . Nobody cares. . . ."

I was thinking it to myself, and I cannot tell you to this day whether or not I actually said those words aloud. All I can say for sure is that Warden Duffy was looking into my eyes with an expression that few men are privileged to see. The thief on the other cross, the one who repented, must have seen a Face like that when he cried out in his agony.

When he spoke, I knew at last that my long descent had ended. My life was not over. It was just beginning. He called me by my first name. And the only thing he said was:

"Bill—*I care.*"

Several days later my cell door was unlocked and I was released from The Shelf. The Jute Mill was waiting for me. Along with my release order, Warden Duffy had left a message with the sergeant.

"The only way to proceed from place to place here is to earn your way—either up or down. You earned your way to Solitary. Now, let's see if you can earn your way out of the Jute Mill."

The Jute Mill was waiting, but its evil snickering was gone. I had something real, something other than self-pity, to think about. Time, the unmoving axis of every convict's existence, began for me to pick up speed.

The days on The Shelf after Warden Duffy's visit had given me a chance to reflect, without interruption. (Somewhere in every human being there should be a Shelf where he can isolate himself and think things through alone.)

"Never make a big decision emotionally," my father had once said.

"It would take a tremendous amount of fixing. . . ." Warden Duffy had said.

Thus I came to realize I could not fix "things"—that is, circumstances outside myself. The prison and all of its component parts would go on with or without me. The outside world had managed for some months now without benefit of my presence. In order to straighten out, it was necessary for me to understand what was wrong—with me. Up to now, everyone else had been to blame. "They" had broken my heart. "She" had beaten me and lied to me. "He" had ignored me. "They" had taken my money, stripped my car. "The system" at Preston was unfair. "The private school" was embarrassed; "the cops" had a bum beef; "Howard" was a stool pigeon; "the bulls" had beaten me. Everything and everybody but me had been at fault. I had been the center of the world, and all circumstances and all people had been reacting to me. As far as I was concerned, no other entities had lives, motives, hopes of their own.

At first it was everybody, and then it was nobody. Nobody cared. But that was no longer true. It was nothing I had forced from anyone at gunpoint. It had been given to me, with open hand and open heart. It was mine if I wanted it. All I had to do was take it. I could start with this.

My thoughts went in obvious succession. There was the second logical step. ("Watch that first step, it's a son of a bitch. If you can make that, then you'll be all right." The quotation flew into my mental processes from somewhere.) The next step was self-questioning. If I had been wrong about whether anyone cared, couldn't I have been wrong before that time—about other things? Wasn't it true that many persons had been unfairly treated and still had not created circumstances to send them to prison? Hadn't some men risen to genuine greatness by overcoming terrible adversity? Take the man who was President of the United States now; hadn't he been struck down with an almost fatal blow of crippling illness? Couldn't *he* have withdrawn into the shell of wealth and "done his own time?" I had heard that Warden Duffy's father had been a prison guard. Perhaps life hadn't been so easy for Duffy when he was a kid, getting an education and a job during the Depression.

I had all of the questions. But, it seemed to me, none of the answers. Well, somewhere the answers existed. Somewhere great men who had found them had set them down in print. I had to discover them in order to find myself and my problems.

The lives and circumstances of great human beings flashed before my mind's eye. Lincoln, Jack London, Helen Keller—all had overcome massive handicaps. John C. Frémont and Alexander Hamilton had been born out of wedlock, yet streets, parks, communities and institutions of learning proudly bear their names. George Washington Carver, born into slavery, had an uninspired beginning. But all of these men had somehow reacted positively; they had regarded obstacles as challenges. Their very hardships seemed to have triggered them to greatness.

Hitler. The synonym for evil flashed across my mind. He had felt put upon and ill-treated. My God! Hitler had reacted the way I had.

Negatively. He had been in prison, too. He had determined to get even with everyone he thought was against him. He called his shots in verbose, vituperative and vitriolic words, spewing out *Mein Kampf.* When he came out of prison, he was determined to get even with the whole world. Right now, in September 1941, it looked as if he might make it.

It behooved me to get answers. To understand how to get better, to accomplish the "fixing," I needed to understand how I became this way, where my reactions had been wrong, what drove me to such extremes. Only then could I change and learn to react as I wanted to.

Motivated by these thoughts, I enrolled in the University of California extension courses that were advertised on the prison bulletin board and in our weekly newspaper. The courses had been available and advertised all along, but for the first time I began to see something in the world besides my own squirrelly self.

The first load of study assignments staggered me. In my effort to discover what made mankind tick—and me along with it—I had enrolled in beginning psychology, philosophy and comparative religions. A long list of books to be covered in the course of instruction was augmented by required outside reading and suggested material. All were available from either the prison library or the University. Degrees, grades, class standings interested me not at all. What I was after were answers. It was a matter of survival.

Survival! It was a burr under my tail. It drove me as few men are driven. Then it came to me. Mankind, both as individuals and as nations, makes its greatest strides forward under the impetus of just such a burr. When men or nations think they have it made, progress stops and retrogression sets in. Not because anyone says so, but because it is the nature of things. Take that burr away, and they sit down and go soft.

This new-found mental horsepower also solved my constrictive time schedule. At first it appeared impossible for me to do eight hours a day in the Jute Mill and still extract what I had to from those demanding courses. Every man working in the prison had an assigned amount of work to perform each week. Completing his work was called "making task," and when this was accomplished he was free to spend the remainder of the work week enjoying the facilities of the library, the athletic field or visiting with fellow convicts in the Main Yard.

I became an inspired jute weaver. I could not have rattled off words fast enough to keep pace with the now frantic tempo of my loom. I would "make task" by Wednesday evening, thus giving me Thursdays and Fridays for study.

There were a few other convict students, and we naturally gravitated together, usually along the base of one wall in the Main Yard where the concrete bastion kept the prevailing shore breeze from frisking with our papers. Discussion proved helpful and, as a result, snatches of unlikely conversations could be overheard in passing.

"Genes and chromosomes dictate the anfractuosities of the brain just as surely as they dictate the color of the eyes. . . ." declared a bespectacled man who had blown safes for a living.

"Not entirely, my learned compatriot. Individual development of the brain increases the convolutions and it has been shown conclusively that the intelligence quotient can be improved. . . ." interrupted a hijacker.

Most men, even as I, insisted upon relating their studies to themselves. The third man, whose avocation had been setting fire to places he had burglarized, interjected:

"That's just what I told her. I sez 'That kid ain't mine—genetics prove that two brown-eyed people can't have a blue-eyed kid. Anyway, you t'ink I can't count? I been up here ten months, and I was in the county jail for five weeks before that. You tryin' to kid me you're an elephant or somepin'?"

Further down the line, a purse-snatcher dismissed a famous piece of military strategy with: "What did them Trojans expect to find in that horse—dames?"

"Yeah," answered the wit of the group, "but that would make it a horse of ill repute."

My studies were absorbing. I plunged into the beliefs of Aristotle, Plato, Confucius, Christ, Mohammed, Freud, Jung. . . . But prison was still prison. I was in it. It was in me. As I struggled to accomplish what religionists might call a rebirth, I could look up from my studies in the corner of the yard and survey the surroundings in which this new life was to be launched. My womb.

I was likely to see a big jocker committing a brutal act of sodomy on his punk standing up against a wall.

Always in view were a number of the seriously mentally ill, some talking to themselves, others standing and staring silently by the hour. Still others would suddenly harangue the unyielding wall with screams:

"Jesus saves. Jesus saves. He that believeth in the Lord . . . Oh, my God, my God, why hast Thou forsaken me?"

There was a little man who spent all his time hanging around the urinal trough, occasionally dipping his fingers into the liquid and rubbing it through his hair. His head, in addition to quantities of urine, held a 5-place table of logarithms and their conversions. This creature could solve the most complex mathematical and engineering problems in less time than it would take to run them through a computer.

There were always a number of "queens" in sight—the truly effeminate men with small bones and facial features, severely belted waists and mincing walks—male only technically. Almost invariably they were paired off with "husbands." Whenever a queen was on the loose, it was short-lived, and there was hell to pay until she was safely "married" again.

Frequently a solicitor could be seen, his punk kneeling behind him, offering, surreptitiously, to sell the unfortunate creature's services to any passerby.

More killings, knifings, bandaged heads and general bloodshed resulted from situations involving queens and punks than from all other causes put together.

If this sounds exciting, it is misleading. These things happen, but they happen quietly, furtively, sullenly. The men do their time with very little comment or conversation. Fighting makes a man lose his time off for good behavior (wherein he can serve as little as three years and nine months on a 5-year sentence). So there are no curses or insults—such as would lead to fistfights on the outside. There are no fistfights. If the issue is worth beefing about, it is done silently and quickly with a knife or a length of pipe. There is a small scuffle, a man lies bleeding; there is the clatter of a shiv or pipe being kicked away. If the weapon is ever found, it is not "on" anyone. There are no fingerprints. That is all.

Everywhere, every minute—like the air you breathe—there is the threat of violence lurking beneath the surface. Unlike the air, it is heavy, massive, as oppressive as molasses. It permeates every second of everyone's existence—the potential threat of sudden, ferocious annihilation. It is as grey and swift and unpredictable as a shark and just as unvocal. There is no letup from it—ever.

With it, however, comes an animal wariness that imparts the appearance of calmness and indifference. Yet it is the prickling watchfulness of a hungry wildcat or a prodded cobra.

Hardly a conducive place for study, one might surmise. But help in strange forms came to me from out of that grey jungle. One day I looked up to see a massive figure making its way, unmistakably, toward me. A path opened voluntarily for him, for bearing down on me was, indisputably, the toughest con in the joint.

He was Bob Welles. A 4-time loser, doing life for murder, without possibility of parole. Legends about him were legion. He had been in the county jail the last time I was there and had teased Howard, my erstwhile crime partner turned canary, into gibbering hysteria by brandishing a spoon and offering to "carve some stool-pigeon pie." I knew Bob and liked him, as I did several other bad boys of San Quentin. Bad, but solid. I had, at first, been drawn naturally to this group. Recently, however, my studies had taken all my free time. As the huge man approached I wondered if he thought I had turned my back on the clique of tough, solid cons. But my animal wariness, which I had learned to trust more than any other faculty, told me there was no danger here.

"Bill-boy." My own sizable hand was lost in his great black paw. "Hear you been studyin'."

"That's right. Studying hard." There was a long pause as the huge solid-muscled Colossus worked to put his thoughts into sentences. Talking came hard for him.

"Someday you oughta be getting out—and if you do, then you oughta stay out."

I waited in silence.

"You listen to my words, Bill-buddy, 'cause I don't often come out with 'em." Since this was true, I paid strict attention with as much respect for the effort that he was making as curiosity about his motives.

With one great blunt finger, he tapped the book I had been reading.

"Schoolin' ain't the whole story, 'cause if it was, you wouldn't be here in the fust place. But you got somethin' besides schoolin' and it's good—if it don't kill you." He pointed to his own face. "Now look at me a minute, boy. Take a good, long look. . . ."

I obeyed. Only by rigid self-control could I keep my face expressionless. The big Negro was a shambling remnant of a tremendous physique, a battered engine of endless vitality and strength. His naturally prominent frontal bones were humped and swollen from blows, protruding so that his eyes were almost obscured. His wide nose literally had been pounded into his face, broken more than a hundred times, torn and mutilated until it was a declivity instead of a protuberance, looking like the end of a double-barrelled shotgun. As he spoke, snaggly broken teeth were visible in a mouth surrounded by scar tissue that obliterated the original lip line. But worst of all was the frightful, liver-colored scar that clove his face diagonally. Half an inch wide in places, it ran from his forehead, down across the place where his nose had been, over cheek and jawline.

"You wanna look like this, huh?"

I couldn't help uttering a low-voiced, embarrassed "No."

"Well, you better make up your mind then. 'Cause you gonna look like this sure as you standin' there if you don't stay out after you once make it out." In his earnestness, Welles gripped my upper arm in one bear-trap hand.

"That's 'cause you tough, Bill. Real tough. Most guys who think they tough—they not tough, they just mean. But you tough, boy. I'm tough and bad both, but I ain't never been just plain mean. And, boy, you gonna go the same way I done if they ever get you in a joint again. 'Cause the only way anyone ever gonna break you is kill you. You know it, and they know it, too. Now that's good on the outside—it's good when you're bein' good. But in here it's murder —and murder is what I mean.

"Before Warden Duffy, my stretches before this here one, them bulls left me for dead many a time. So fur, I always got up again. But someday when they leave ol' Bob for dead, that's just what he'll be. You, too, boy. Lessen you stay outa joints and quit lookin' up to men like me.

"I'll tell you this—bein' the toughest con in the joint don't make the time no easier. I gets awful . . . lonesome. . . ."

Then he was gone. But that soft, deep voice has come back to me many times since—times when it may have made the difference. I looked down at the book in my hand. I had been reading that Christ had said every man had His Divine spark. So for counsel that has lasted me all my life since—and for the Spark that prompted that tough old con to quit "doing his own time" long enough to give it —I offer my belated thanks to Bob Welles.

I went back to my books. There were new and fascinating worlds in them. The sayings and discoveries of the ancients were old as time itself, but all new to me—as, indeed, were Freud and Jung, their followers and interpretations of their works; Will James and his great chapters on habit; the field of concepts and action; the sub-conscious, the sensor band between it and the conscious mind.

I concluded that I did not have, as I had believed, actual free choice in my decisions. Those decisions were made long ago, some in infancy, many in childhood. From stimuli of various kinds, shock, humor, pain and other experiences during those impressionable years, my concepts had been formed.

Later, it was not a matter of deciding whether I would coldheart-edly go with my father, stow away, fight brutally, hit a man with a shovel when his back was turned or strike another with a pistol butt when he lay unresisting and helpless, rob at gunpoint, terrify honest people and deprive them of what was rightfully theirs. The con-cepts I had, lying in wait in my subconscious mind, reacted in one way—the negative way—to stimuli of all kinds and pushed my ideas from the subconscious back across the conscious mind and into the field of action.

The action was wrong because the conscious thought was wrong because the concept was wrong.

But how does one go about changing concepts that are buried beneath the sensor band? How could I even find out what they were? Answers to these two imponderables finally began to emerge of their own accord. I would examine some specific misbehavior of mine in the past. Then I would figure out what concept triggered that particular action. The next step was to figure out what action I should have taken instead. The "right" action—the action I now preferred to take. I had to discover what the concept should have been to precipitate the correct move. It was painstaking, repetitive, mind-cracking work and demanded great powers of concentration, more than I dared hope to possess.

My studies showed that criminal actions are not the real seat of the trouble. They are but the symptoms of a deeper disturbance. Some criminals, of course, are actually psychotic. But so are many non-criminals. My own problems were nothing I could blame on outside influence. Laying off blame is no help, only delaying or cancelling the day of recognition of the real fault. My problems stemmed from my reactions to my experiences. And regardless of what the experiences were or where the original fault lay, I finally admitted that the problem was within me. I must go there to fix it. Inward. Alone.

Figuring this out was merely groundwork for the job ahead. There were many times I thought I never would "make task" on this one. But I had to. It was a matter of survival.

Suddenly it seemed as if my studies were beginning to pay off. I was no longer in the Jute Mill. The tedium that I had endured for six months was gone. Gone forever, I determined.

With no advance notification I was sent to the education department and instructed to brush up on my typing. I regained my old speed quickly and even improved on it. Then I was transferred again. To the administration building . . . outside the walls.

There was the bay with its whitecaps and little raw-red earthen islands and the wheeling gulls above and the green hills fading to smoky blue across the water. It wasn't until the bull accompanying me nudged me with his cane that I realized the unexpected sight had halted me in my tracks.

Minutes later I learned there was need for skilled typists in the office of the Clerk of the Parole Board. I was taken to the second floor of the building and was assigned the desk next to a young convict who was typing at a tremendous rate of speed. The bull told me this man would explain my duties. Although I did not recognize the other cons doing desk work, I knew the man next to me to be a member of the "tough and solid" clique of the yard. He was called "Hook," presumably because of his overly large, broken nose. After the bull left, Hook stopped typing.

"So you have the second-highest I.Q. in the joint!" This was his salutation. He looked quizzically at me.

"I didn't know that. How do you know it?"

"Meet number one." His face was transformed by a homely, friendly grin as he held out his hand.

"We're only two points apart," he said, as we shook hands. Then, indicating the pile of manila folders on his desk, he explained:

"All that info is contained in these records. You're not up for parole consideration now, as you doubtless are aware." Another grin, "But the grapevine had it that you were being assigned here, so I looked you up."

Hook explained that we were to type stencils from the records. Because typing stencils is much more exacting than regular typing, I wondered if I would ever attain anything like his speed. When the work day was ended, he was stacks ahead of me. Then he, the other cons and I were marched back inside the walls for the evening meal.

But there was still another change in store that day. I was told to collect my personal effects from my cell; my sleeping quarters were being transferred. I shook hands with Barney and followed the bull to a portion of the prison known as the Old Spanish Cellblock, a section of the original adobe edifice constructed in the 1870's. I was directed to one of the dormitories, each set up for occupancy by sixteen men. The dormitory at Preston had seemed forbidding, but after San Quentin's 2-man barred cell, this one looked good. Here three large rooms were connected by low archways. Plumbing had been installed. We could shower every day instead of only twice a week.

I knew most of the cons here and saw that Hook was just moving in, too. He told me he had been on the job in the "Ad" building only two days before me. I was amazed at the competency he had achieved in such a short time. It developed later that he was quite an amazing man. But even he didn't know that on that winter evening in 1942 when we selected bunks that were side by side in the dormitory of the Old Spanish Cellblock. It was after we had showered and were almost asleep that Hook said:

"Wilber. Wilber Power Sewell. That's a hell of a name. What do they call you—Will Power?"

"Call me *Bill*," I instructed him firmly. "I don't even know your name, outside of 'Hook.'" I was dozing off and barely heard his sleepy reply.

"Chessman—Caryl Chessman."

5

NOW MY DAYS PASSED SWIFTLY. I WORKED
in an office with a pleasant view from an
unbarred window. Chess, as I came to call
him, made task by Wednesday afternoon.
But instead of taking off, he would help
me complete my work so we could both
take off on Thursday. We became good
friends. In our off-duty hours we formed
the San Quentin Debating Team, which
met and defeated many university squads.
When I thought up a radio playhouse for
presentation of dramatic skits over the
prison network, it was Chess who pitched
in, doing most of the writing.

Together, we discussed many things, including the work I was trying to do on my concepts. It was an invaluable help to have a confidante with such a quick, facile mind and genuine sense of humor. One day, as we stood in the Main Yard, I was preoccupied with my concept of an ideal wife: an intelligent woman, one who could also be termed "solid," and who would understand the mental work involved in rehabilitation. I was in deep thought when I realized Chess was speaking to me.

"What's bothering you?" he asked.

"I was thinking how tough it will be for me to find the right wife," I answered seriously, expecting his usual, ready empathy.

"Offhand," said Chess, waving at the Main Yard, "I would say you could not have chosen a more difficult place in which to locate your soul mate."

In our private talks, Chess argued that he considered it a sign of superior intelligence to operate, successfully, outside the law. His chosen route was to declare war on authority or coercion of any kind. He had been to Preston twice. He said crime fulfilled his yen for excitement. I contended excitement could be obtained within the law, but it seemed to me the more we debated the issue the more firmly each of us hewed to his own viewpoint.

Chess was headed one way and I another. But it would be less than accurate for me to tell this without stating, unequivocally, that the Caryl Chessman I knew so well from 1941 until he was transferred out of San Quentin in 1943, convicted of armed robbery, was a man physically, mentally and emotionally incapable of committing the sex crimes for which he was eventually tried and executed.

Members of an all-male society do talk about sex, you know. Exhaustively. Chess's ideas, experiences and aspirations were on a par with those of the other solid cons who form the backbone of any prison population—normal, healthy and not overly imaginative. When you live with a man twenty-four hours a day for almost two years in the close confinement of a prison, you get to know him far better than most men know their brothers. And if someone tells you your brother is a sex deviate, you damn well know whether he is or not.

Caryl Chessman was no sex deviate. Not then, not ever. He

shared not only with me but with the vast majority of the men in prison, the contempt and disgust for rapos, punks and jockers.

Rapists, contrary to the accepted beliefs of many on the "outside," who have never had to share total confinement with them, are not big, strong, lusty men. They are usually weak creatures, basically scared to death of women. Many of them do not know there is such a thing as sex with consent. They do not understand courting, in the normal sense of the word. Still they have sex drives that they relieve by attack and force, sometimes killing their victims after raping them in order to escape detection or frequently killing their victims before in order to accomplish the rape.

I do not pretend to understand the warped minds of such creatures, but I do know they are basically weak, frightened individuals, lacking character, charm, persuasiveness or any quality a woman might find attractive.

Chessman was the exact opposite in every way. He had a strong personality and a brilliant mind. His resourcefulness and persuasion are now a matter of worldwide knowledge and perhaps a specific and stinging memory to the individuals who finally accomplished his execution. Accomplished it, I might add, without ever allowing him the lie-detector tests he sought for twelve years and which, he declared, would prove his innocence.

The following six months in San Quentin were "easy time" compared to the slow and agonizing initial half year in the Jute Mill. My studies and my work were enough to keep me busy, but in addition there were the debating team, the radio theater and "San Quentin on the Air," the new weekly program broadcast across the nation. Warden Duffy always made a brief talk and usually emphasized the importance of rehabilitation. I had the privilege of acting as the prison master of ceremonies.

I turned 21 and hoped I was truly coming of age. I had made my first appearance before the parole board and, as expected, was denied consideration.

But while much had transpired inside, I felt the outside world was going on without us. Our country was now at war. There had been great excitement and rumors after the bombing of Pearl Harbor. There was wild talk of convict "suicide squads" and impending Japanese air raids on the West Coast. Warden Duffy and his wife had gone on the prison network at that time, squelching the rumors and settling some of the unrest. Now, aside from the occasional visits of the Red Cross blood bank, it was apparent that the war was going to be won or lost without us.

It seemed to me, as I sat there with my books at the base of the wall in the Main Yard that summer afternoon in 1942, that the war-generated unrest had never quite been dissipated. But I had other things on my mind.

For more than a year now, the toughest part of my existence had stemmed from the fact that I received no letters since my father's death. I had never received a letter from my mother, although I wrote three times a week to her. The farther I got away from the bitterness in my thinking, the more difficult this situation became to live with. Every single great truth I had discovered in my studies showed the futility and danger of holding grudges and resentments. Doors will not open, for a mind that harbors ill will or hatred. The cold bitterness that had once filled my heart and consciousness was gone. I only wanted her to know that—to recognize the fact I had realized my wrongdoing and was working hard to become better. This was what I wanted—at first.

Later I was willing to settle for less. Finally, for the first and last time in my life, I grovelled before another human being. I begged for just one card, a Christmas card, a birthday card—not both, just one or the other, and not every year, only one and only once. That's all I asked for. Just to let me know there was someone on the outside, one person who knew I wasn't all bad . . . that I was trying. . . . No, I didn't ask even that anymore . . . all I begged for now was that someone knew I was alive.

There was no answer. No card. Nothing. Ever.

So it was that afternoon as I sat in the Main Yard, dwelling on my aloneness. The whole place seemed to reflect my mood. It reflected more than just its usual scowling, brooding self. It was restive, tight; there wasn't a man who couldn't feel it. It rang an alarm bell in the minds of the con-wise.

What threat was about to be unleashed I didn't know. Never would know. For at this moment something else happened—in the yard and in me—that was to influence me profoundly for the remainder of my life.

From the other end of the Yard came a sound that could mean only one thing. Warden Duffy was among us. The waves of applause told me his location. Worried, I hopped up on one of the benches next to the wall to get a vantage point.

He had probably jumped up and left his desk, the way he often did, and gone off with something preoccupying his mind. He had a habit of starting out suddenly, without warning. It had been at first the only way he could ferret out wrongdoing. Now here he was, with only good on his mind, walking into this yard at this precise moment when something big was brewing and anyone's existence could be cut short without warning.

Even the usual sound of applause bouncing back and forth in this huge concrete echo chamber, didn't reassure me. Sure we liked him, trusted him, didn't want to see anything happen to him— for selfish reasons if no other. This was true of those of us who were in our right minds. But how about the psychos, lost forever in their private worlds behind walls of which there was no penetrating? Sometimes one would run berserk—slashing, gouging, kicking, even biting anyone in his path. Just before I arrived at San Quentin, one such creature, amuck and foaming at the mouth, was shot to death by one of the gun bulls just as a mad dog is shot down.

And how about the non-psychos who might suddenly decide that Warden Duffy was the personification of some hated regulation? As in every organization made up of a large number of human beings, there were injustices here, because human beings make mistakes—in paper work, in judgment and in their relations with each other. But the reaction here was, invariably, far different than that encountered elsewhere. Almost every act was taken as a personal affront and was dealt with violently.

There were many men in the yard who were murderers. There were enough knives hidden among them to stock a cutlery warehouse. There were men who, literally, could not do any more time—to whom the gas chamber beckoned more invitingly than a dive from the top tier. There was the infrequent, but not unheard of, escape plot—and what better hostage than the Warden to assure a way out? The Main Yard always had its quota of those who had abandoned all hope and to whom killing had lost all meaning and reality.

I had seen Warden Duffy pass through the crowds of men before, but this time I was worried, helpless and afraid for him. As the men pressed about him, cheering, applauding, calling his name, the crush overwhelmed him to the point where he was beyond any hope of help from watchful eyes and guns above or from any other human source.

But the mood of the Yard was broken, unmistakably, conclusively. The rumbling volcano that had been shaking all of us had turned to ice. This was no story, however convincingly recounted, that I had received secondhand. It was no fanciful movie that caught my imagination only to drop me again when the theater lights came on. I was part of it. Whatever it was that happened in the Main Yard of San Quentin that day, happened in me.

All I can say for sure is that I knew suddenly there was no cause for concern about Warden Duffy, or about anything while he was there. The prickling went out of my skin; the animal wariness relaxed. The psychos ceased their ranting and muttering. The little creature of the logarithms stopped his everlasting dabbling and stood quietly beside the trough. Big Bob Welles slouched comfortably against the wall, head back, the furtive, ever watchful animal eyes closed—and napped.

What had produced this? Out of the thousands of men in the big yard, there were, literally, hundreds who were not responsible for their actions. And hundreds so bitter, so tough, so institutionalized that no laws, no punishment, nothing society had ever been able to devise could hold them in check. What held them in check now?

What I saw was impossible. Not just because I say so, but because it had been impossible in all the years of San Quentin's existence for a warden to walk unescorted into that Main Yard when it was occupied. Most of the men present had been here before Warden Duffy. He didn't get a new group of men to start in with "fresh," along with his own new and progressive ideas.

It is damned tough to accept the impossible as fact, even when you are living through it. I would certainly have discarded the evidence of my own eyes if it had not happened time after time. I saw it and I felt it. Therefore, I had to believe it. Besides, there is the official prison record of it. More important, there is the unwritten record of it as a bright and wondrous thing in the memories of thousands of men.

At the very least, what we witnessed and were a part of daily, was —by definition—a miracle. Of course, the Red Sea could open, a Man could walk on the water, the blind could see and the dead get up and walk if this could happen. There is no big or small to a miracle. It is a happening beyond man's understanding of natural laws.

How?

The answers fairly leaped out of my readings.

". . . *the world is plastic to your thoughts* . . ."

"*If your faith be as a grain of mustard* . . ."

"*Perfect love casteth out all fear* . . ."

These sayings had to do with religion. But there were also hard, objective scientific data that did not clash with these spiritual concepts. Records of experiments in psychokinesis at Duke University and elsewhere show that plants, animals, people and even inanimate objects can be controlled by the human mind.

I was privileged to witness a tangible living proof that these teachers were dealing in facts, not theory.

Faith was the answer. Belief. Trust. Warden Duffy's unshakable faith in the spark of goodness inherent in every man. He reaffirmed it on the radio, in the newspapers, to the State legislature. His credo was that punishment alone was not enough; it must be accompanied by enlightenment and rehabilitation.

If he could do this literally impossible task, couldn't I, by applying the same principles, do something for myself? The religious teachers said so. The science records said so. And far more eloquently, my own eyes told me so. The answer was built into the question.

Faith was my only hope for freedom. I was still under indeterminate sentence—one of these days my time would be set—very possibly at ninety-nine years. After that, I could apply for parole. I had no money to hire a lawyer and my father's friends—many in high places —all blamed me for his death. Any contact between them and the Parole Board would have a deleterious effect upon my future. Since all usual agencies were ruled out by these circumstances, it was obvious some unusual agencies would have to be brought to bear.

As I lay in bed that night, I was so restless that Chess finally sat up in his bed and asked me if I were sick.

"No, just the opposite," I told him. "I am thinking about a miracle. . . ."

"That certainly clears up any question I might have had on my mind," he retorted dryly. "There is only one miracle that could happen around here that would interest me in the slightest and that would be to see the bars drop off of that window and the Front Gate swing open."

"That's the one I'm working on."

All night my mind kept revolving around Warden Duffy and his slow progress through the Yard. It was slowed because of the crush of men with questions and requests that only the Warden could solve. For he was the only one the cons trusted with their personal problems.

"My mother came here from the East to see me. She has to go back before the next visiting day. . . . Couldn't she come in tomorrow?"

"Warden, my brother's been drafted and that leaves my two kid sisters alone. Can't they get some kind of relief or something, the county won't . . ."

"My wife sent me a pen and pencil set and it's been held up in the office for three weeks. They say I can't have it 'cause I already have one. But it's broke. . . ."

And always that kindly voice would reply:

"Put your name and number on a piece of paper and two or three words about your question. Hand it back to me and I'll take care of it." Over and over the same words to each man who came up. "I'll see to it. I'll take care of it—I promise. You have my word. I'll do it."

By the time he returned to his office, he would have scores, sometimes hundreds, of scraps of paper, match covers, pages torn from books and even little wisps of cigarette papers, each with name, number and urgent plea scrawled thereon. Word had gone along the grapevine that the Warden would examine each scrap and set to work dictating replies, issuing special visiting passes, telephoning the property office or making whatever effort it took to fulfill "I'll see to it—I'll take care of it—I promise." Nor did he ever leave his office that night until all the papers collected that day had been taken care of. Sometimes it took until after midnight. Warden Duffy didn't merely tell men about their responsibility to others. He demonstrated it—every day of his life.

As soon as I reached the Administration Building the next morning, I asked the Warden's convict secretary for an appointment with him. Then I went upstairs to try to concentrate on my work. For once I had told Chess nothing of what was on my mind.

When I was sent for, the convict secretary ushered me in and closed the door. Interview time with Warden Duffy was exactly what he promised—private and confidential.

By a fitting coincidence, the Warden's desk top was covered with small bits of paper. Everything seemed to be falling into place.

"Well, Bill, what can I do for you?" The Warden motioned me to a chair.

"I hope I can do something for you—for a change." I was committed. "I have an idea that might help you with all these requests and probably more that don't reach you—and you wouldn't have to go through all this."

"Would it satisfy the men just as well, too?" Trust the Warden to put that first. His face showed only warmth and interest, no skepticism. "What is your idea, Bill?"

"I thought we could set up question boxes—locked question boxes—in the cellblocks, the Main Yard and the mess hall, inviting everybody to drop in their requests. Then, you could answer them once a week on the prison radio network. We could make an interesting program by using interview form, with me doing the asking, in the words and tone the guys would use, and you answering it as if you were talking to each man personally. You must get a lot of the same questions. This would save you having to answer the same ones over and over, by answering it once. I think the cons would be interested and feel included.

"I'm talking about matters of general interest to everyone. There are some prison policies we don't think are fair. How about a chance to argue it? There are still all sorts of rumors about the war—every batch of fish in the gate brings another flock of them. Guys who work in the Jute Mill have made a couple of good suggestions to increase efficiency. But they haven't been put into practice.

"The South Cellblock was shaken down from stem to stern last week, every cell taken apart, private property torn up and God knows what. The guards didn't find anything. What were they looking for? How about things like that?

"Of course, the things about pen sets and visiting days are not of general interest. The very private matters some of the men ask about, you could answer in the same way you always have. But I really think that such a program could be very helpful and also save you a lot of work and duplication."

Warden Duffy took his eyes from mine and looked over the little scraps on his desk.

"There ought to be a better way for the men to communicate their problems—something with a little more dignity. I care about how the men feel as well as just answering the problem of the moment. I care. . . ." he said.

"We could call it 'Interview Time with Warden Duffy.' There are only two things. . . ."

His interest had quickened. "And those are?"

"The question boxes should be padlocked. There should be only one key—and I should have it. That's to do away with the possibility of any interference by the scr—the guards—and to keep stool-pigeon letters from reaching you."

"What would you do with letters from informers?" The Warden never used any of the convict expressions.

"I'm not sure yet," I answered truthfully. "Except to keep them from reaching you. If the boxes ever were known as stool-pigeon drops, the men would stay away from them like poison and probably end up by staging a bonfire with them.

"But, sir, if you were to go on the radio before we started the program and give your word to the men that I was to have the only key, they'd believe you. They would know I'd see the contents of the boxes first and that would automatically keep any stoolies from getting into the act."

(Nobody likes a stool pigeon, but wardens and policemen have to act upon information given to them this way.)

"The way I see it, sir, it would be like management and labor sitting down to negotiate. The men would know they always had a representative pitching for them. It should make for better understanding between the men and the State and—it's something I think all the men would appreciate. I'm sure I would."

The Warden was deeply thoughtful. "It sounds all right, Bill. I'm going to give it more thought. You'll have my answer tomorrow."

That night, when I was even more restless than the previous night, my perceptive friend Chess whispered from his bed:

"What the hell did you ask him for—a machine gun?"

The following morning, the Warden said, "I think your proposal is a fine one, Bill. I mentioned it to Mrs. Duffy, and she agrees. It looks like a full-time job to me."

It was. I was given my own small office, and even with full concentration, it took fourteen to sixteen hours a day to get it organized and, later, to keep it going.

But "Interview Time with Warden Duffy" was a success. From my early, hectic days in the prison, the cons knew I was solid. Therefore, it received their wholehearted cooperation and did what it was intended to do—create better understanding between the inmates and the State. As a result, several improvements in prison routine were inaugurated. The program was also credited with lifting wartime morale, which had been in a slump. Warden Duffy saw none of the occasional stool-pigeon letters. They were handled in such a way as to discourage the authors and not embarrass the administration. The venture far surpassed my original idea of saving the Warden time. Newspapers outside the prison wrote warmly about it, and one spokesman for the State called it a "very worthwhile contribution in the field of penology."

Then, one day, I nearly lost my life. The circumstances that saved it were to have a far-reaching effect on me. It happened early one evening as I hurried along on some errand for the radio program. It was nearly dark and the Main Yard was almost deserted. Intent on my thoughts, I had lost my customary wariness. Suddenly, I heard the clatter of a shiv on the concrete behind me. It was followed by the sound of a scuffle.

As I wheeled around, I saw one of my tough, solid friends, Red, locked in a right unloving embrace with a stranger, a fish. Red brought his knee up. The other man relaxed and slumped to the pavement with a groan. Red's shirt was turning red. He held his hand to his chest, sighed heavily and sat down suddenly.

"What the hell happened?" I tore open my friend's shirt. The gash was painful, but not, I correctly surmised, fatal.

". . . wasn't time to yell or nothin'. He had that shiv goin' straight for your back, Bill," he gasped. We ripped up his shirt to make a bandage.

For Red to have knifed the man himself or to have shouted a warning, even belatedly, would have been understandable. It was to be expected from a tough, solid con friend. But neither the convict code nor any other would have demanded a man to take a knife in his chest for a friend. I owed him a great debt, one I'd be happy to repay if he ever needed me. As I tried to mumble something to this effect, Red waved it aside.

"That program you've got goin' with the Warden is really doin' some good," he said. "I just didn't wanna miss the next one."

As the program began to exert more influence, it required more time, thought and discussion with the Warden. As a result, he moved our broadcast booth to his home on the hill behind the Administration Building. We spent every Friday evening there, first going over what was to be used, then conducting the program and, later, hashing over proposed improvements for the following week. I also consulted with him there on evenings when his duties kept me from seeing him in his office. That is how I met Mrs. Duffy.

A feminine counterpart of her husband, she was well known to us cons as a staunch backer of all his progressive ideas. She was as vitally interested in the inner workings of San Quentin as he, and she was frequently seen with him in the Main Yard, in the mess hall, even sitting in the darkened movie showings. Further concrete proof of his faith—and hers—in the men.

From the first time Mrs. Duffy met me at the door of their home with a warm, "Well, at last. . . . Do come in, Bill, I've been looking forward to meeting you for so long," I knew something else, too. My upbringing had taught me to recognize a lady when I met one. And here was a lady.

Our first broadcast from the Duffy home came at Christmastime, and I asked her to say a few words on the air. She spoke for less than a minute, but I think every man in the joint felt a little better because of the few warm phrases from a cultured feminine voice.

That first evening and subsequent ones I was careful and restrained. I thought every sentence through before I voiced it. I had relearned the art of handling delicate china teacups and the thick rug had become familiar underfoot before I was sure that the fearful obscenities that are a part of every con's normal, everyday language would not creep into my conversations in this home.

It took a while to break down my reserve, not because of distrust, but because I was in the habit of being a con's con, solid, forceful, grim, doing my own time. Warden Duffy understood. The Duffys met me about halfway, not wanting to hurry either me or themselves. But gradually our conversations branched out beyond the radio program. We had many stimulating discussions on philosophy, religion, analyzing the forces that drive people to violence, wrongdoing and drink. We searched for qualities men must have in order to be good. I was anxious to hear everything the Duffys thought about these matters. Not only was it an opportunity for me to discuss the anatomy of faith with people who already had demonstrated so conclusively that they truly possessed it—but it was a matter of the survival of my own mind.

Now, for the first time, I shared with another human being the work I was doing on my concepts—the real, painful, mind-cracking upward climb along the path I hoped (with all the hope I had) would lead to true rehabilitation. I had debated the theory with Chess, but I couldn't unburden myself to him as I could to the Warden and his wife.

To these warm, honest people, who really cared, not only about me, but about everyone inside and outside of prison, I could at last relieve my mind and unload my heart. In time it came out, bit by bit.

This was how it was after I had been in San Quentin two years. During perhaps 5 hours of the 168 hours in the week, I felt more like part of a family, this good family, than I did like a convict. The pendulum within me swung wider, as I had to return from the warmth and gentility of the Duffy home to the world of violence, with its grey pasts and its greyer futures.

But as I left the Duffys on a particular July evening in 1943, after the program, I was thinking of the date I had to keep in the morning —my second hearing before the Parole Board.

Earlier, Mrs. Duffy had brought in the coffee service, as was her custom, and we settled in our usual places—the Warden in his big leather chair, Mrs. Duffy on the couch by the low table and myself in a comfortable chair across from the Warden. For a time, no one spoke. My thoughts were in a turmoil. It had been six weeks since the Warden had spoken about my parole hearing. At that time he had said:

"You have done a lot of fixing, Bill. Now it's my turn to do the recommending. I will. You can count on it." The warmth of that moment had returned many times since. It was with me again. But tonight apparently Warden Duffy's mind was on other things. He was looking at the evening's script. Mrs. Duffy was doing something to the coffee pot. My own coffee remained untouched. Finally, I couldn't stand it any longer.

"Well, Warden, the Parole Board has been in session for two days. My turn comes tomorrow. . . ."

"I know. They will have you before them at about eleven o'clock."

I had been thinking only of tomorrow—The Day. Warden Duffy had it figured down to the exact time.

"You can rest assured I will be there with you." He smiled. "My secretary is to notify me when your number comes up, and I think you know I will do everything within my power for you."

I knew.

"Both Mrs. Duffy and I believe you have reached that psychologically right moment, Bill. . . ."

The telephone interrupted. He went to answer it in the hallway and closed the door. Mrs. Duffy gave me fresh coffee and then, as she had a way of doing, continued with her husband's thought.

"Bill, you were a pretty sick young man when you arrived in San Quentin. The Warden and I both feel you are much better now. It has long been our belief, and our convictions are shared by nearly every leading penologist, that the basic premise used in most prisons is false. Society, its judges and its prisons seem to think only about the punishment that is to be meted out to its offenders. We think criminality is a sickness that needs to be cured, not just punished. Confinement and punishment, too, can play a part in the cure. But the cure, the rehabilitation of men—that should be the main object.

"We do not believe a man should be released from prison until he has rehabilitated himself. To release him before that time is dangerous to society. He might fall into criminal ways again, simply because his sickness has not been cured.

"Neither do we believe a man should be held past the point where he has demonstrated rehabilitation. That is Warden Duffy's objective with all of the men. If an inmate is held too long, he may become bitter and that is as dangerous as releasing him too soon. So you see the vital importance of the 'right' time for release. Both the Warden and I think that, for you, the time has arrived. You've been punished, but more important is the fact you also have been helped."

Her voice broke a little.

"Bill, you've changed to a fine young man and, well, I know you'd never make the Warden take that long walk. . . ." She looked at me almost beseechingly. I didn't understand her last statement.

"What 'long walk'? An execution?"

"Bill, I never talk about executions. You know how we feel about capital punishment." Executions, which law required the Warden to perform, came closer to defeating this strong man than this world will ever know. "No, Bill, I am speaking of men who have been released on the Warden's recommendation. Men he has worked with personally, and for whom he has had high hopes. When one of these men is returned as a parole violator, the Warden goes to see him immediately. He doesn't ask why the man violated his parole. What he wants to know is 'Where did I fail him? How could I have helped him more?' He takes every man's inadequacies as his own personal responsibility. When he comes home to me after one of these visits, he is tired and pale and shaken, almost as much as after an execution. He will say, 'My, it was a long walk over to talk to that man. I'm tired.' "

I could not understand it then. I still cannot understand it. If Warden Duffy had become case-hardened or at least had taken a

"You can't win 'em all" attitude, it would have been much easier for him. But he never has. He has gone on taking each man's failure as his own personal defeat and yet, time and again, he has risen above these defeats to bring life and hope to other men. To Warden Duffy there are no incorrigibles. There are no "good" men and "bad" men—only men who know and men who don't know. He seemed to be able to draw forever on his own reserves to help those who don't know. He had summed it up for me very simply that day when he said, "Bill, I care."

"I've been telling Bill about the psychologically 'right' moment and that we feel he has reached it. I told him also I am depending on him not to let you down," Mrs. Duffy said as the Warden returned.

"We're both depending on it, Bill." He smiled, but he was serious.

"You are depending on me? It's I who am depending on you . . . oh, not just to recommend me for release, but in a way you don't even know about.

"From my reading," I added soberly, "it has become obvious to me that no man can be an island—that premise runs through all the great teachings. Every man must have some hub to revolve around, some keel to go away from and come back to. For me you are that keel. There's more you ought to know, but it's kind of personal."

"Go on, Bill," the Warden urged.

"When I first came here to the house, my feelings for you were a mixture of fear, respect and apprehension. When I began to relax, those feelings grew to admiration and liking and more.

"Everyone has to have somebody. My father is dead and my mother is—well. . . . So I picked you. Without asking you or telling you. You don't have to do anything about it, except go on being what you are. If we could pick our own parents, I would have picked you. I know you don't need me for a son. You have a son studying medicine. But I just thought you should know this is how I feel. I won't let you down. I can't. You are a part of me—the most important part. If, when, I get out, I'll lead my own life. But no matter where I go or what I do, it won't be the kind of life that will put me back into prison again. That is because I'll take this, that I have found here, with me. You will be with me. I love you both. Really love you. I can't imagine life without you. I hope this doesn't upset you, but it's the way I feel and I think you're entitled to know."

I had said it. Now, I could say no more. Mrs. Duffy was the first to speak.

"Bill, it has been pretty obvious how you were beginning to feel about us. We have discussed it several times. Sometimes there are dangers in becoming too closely attached to people, but the Warden and I are proud of the fine progress you have made. Perhaps you'll feel better if, instead of Mrs. Duffy you call me 'Mom' from now on."

"I'll be at the board meeting with you in the morning," the Warden assured me.

"Yes, sir. Thank you. Goodnight, Mom. And goodnight, Warden."

The night air was cool for July. An on-shore breeze was rising. Mom Duffy. I called her that, then, and I do to this day. It fits like a glove. But with Warden Duffy, it was something else. Certainly with no less love, I feel he is the finest man who ever walked the earth. But to me he will always be Warden. My Warden and the Warden of my conscience many times.

He had said he would do everything in his power in the morning. And he did.

When I stood before the Parole Board, five serious-faced men around a long, shining table with manila files on it, Warden Duffy appeared with me (just as my father had in that courtroom two years ago). The Warden addressed the board, movingly, with eloquence.

Some of the words came through my numbed senses, ". . . gave unstintingly of his time to bettering relations between the inmates and the State . . . fourteen and sixteen hours a day . . . this is the true rehabilitation we refer to, but don't often see . . . this is not only a recommendation, gentlemen, this is an opportunity. . . ."

He had stopped speaking. I was dismissed from the room. Warden Duffy stayed on. Another fifteen minutes and he came into the waiting room outside of his office. He handed me a brown sealed envelope. With shaking fingers I tore it open, drew out the pink slip of paper inside.

California State Board of Prisons and Paroles. It was a printed form with only a few blanks for handwritten names and numbers. I read on:

". . . has on this date met and considered the below-captioned case—*Sewell, Wilber Power, 66836, Violation 211, P. C.* and sentence is set at *Fifty (50) Years.*"

My heart stopped.

Below that, on the unfamiliar form, it said:

"Your application for parole is hereby *Granted*. Effective, *October 11, 1943*."

In ninety days I would be free.

It was my last night in San Quentin. The ninety days had passed. "Interview Time" had been replaced by a group of six men who now represented the inmate population. This was the Inmate Council—a system that exists to this day, not only in San Quentin, but in many other prisons throughout the nation.

In the morning, I would be going out. My friend Chess had been transferred to Chino, the minimum security institution near Los Angeles. It was no trick to escape from unwalled Chino, as Chess promptly proved. Yes, Chess had gone, apparently with no apprehensions about the outside world and his future role in it.

Bob Welles was awaiting trial for assaulting a Folsom guard; it was said that he was headed for Death Row. His time was almost over. He, too, knew what he wanted and how to get it.*

Yes, the night of October 10, 1943, I lay in my bunk, wide-awake, smoking and with the taste of freedom strong in my mouth. I had contracted what prison parlance calls "short-time fever."

I thought of old Tony, paroled after thirty-nine years in prison. In less than a week he was back at the Front Gate, begging to be let in. He had found no comfortable place in that strange outside world. He had been allowed back in. Even he knew where he belonged.

But what about me? Where was I going? What was I going to do? What the hell was I, anyway? Me, with my brand new concepts, traits and emotions, all formed in this violent, contradictory womb?

I was a few days past my twenty-third birthday. Every man that age has some twenty years of precedents he can remember—background directing him toward some definite goal. The Duffys' son was studying to be a doctor. If my family had stayed together I would have been working toward my degree in law. I thought about it with-

---

* Robert Welles in early 1964 was still a prison inmate. Once sentenced to death, he was commuted to life in prison and has never been free since.

out regret, merely noting that regardless of what background a man might have, at least it was there. Lawyer or filling-station attendant, it didn't matter. What mattered was that he had accumulated experience and precedents on which to base future judgments, actions and reactions. I had nothing to reach back to in my mind for guidance. My family, and all it represented, was gone, irrevocably, through death and desertion. Wilber Power Sewell, when first heard of, was a brash squirt, mad at the world, refusing to be tamed, resentful, defiant, fighting and useless. That individual had disappeared forever. Whatever made him tick had died behind the walls of San Quentin.

Now, two years and three months later, that number again would be traded for a name. But who was this stranger coming out with that name? I had been born, full-grown, within the walls of San Quentin. *The experiences that had forged this new man hardly were conducive to getting along anywhere but in here.*

My height was more than six-foot-two. I weighed 190 and I could (and had) taken care of myself in beefs that are as rough as they come. But the inner forces that were to make me tick, I had put together myself. I figured my actual emotional age as about twenty months, starting from the time I met Warden Duffy on The Shelf.

Although I had had the wisdom of the ages from which to draw conclusions, they were only theories. The concepts were my own, painfully homemade. Would they hold up under actual use? (One thing I knew for a certainty, however. I would rather die than let down the Duffys.) I was a living anomaly. In order to survive and one day to practice my concepts, I had had to become a part of this most unlikely of societies. A man could conceivably learn from books all there is to know about the internal combustion engine. Yet put him in the driver's seat of a car for the first time and he and the countryside are in for a pretty wild ride.

What it boiled down to was that *here was a manufactured human being, and I was its imperfect creator.*

My very fallibility, however, washed away my apprehensions, leaving only the excitement. Because I was so very far from perfection and so very young, I couldn't help but look forward to that ride.

"Hey, World. Don't stop turning. I want to get on!"

Book Two

6

The Japanese observation plane, circling way up there in a dome of burning blue, looked like a wisp from a burned-out match. The tropical glare burned our eyeballs as we strained for a glimpse of it revolving beyond reach of our antiaircraft, radioing our position to prowling subs.

To keep that resolve to die rather than go back to prison looked easy right now. It was actually beginning to look unavoidable as our unescorted Liberty ship plowed northward in the hostile ocean, a target for subs. Even the tropical night provided no guarantee that we'd escape. But our chances would be a lot better.

"Wish they'd get it over with," said some fish—or whatever they call a green hand in the Merchant Marine. I was green, too, this being my first trip. But I had been in solely masculine company a couple of times before—where it was best to keep your mouth shut and see what happened.

"You wouldn't wish it if you'd ever been torpedoed," came the reply from a craggy able-bodied seaman. "Keep your snotty mouth shut. . . ."

"Let's see you make me. . . ."

"By God, I'll wrap this wrench around your——"

They were off again. Six weeks of this sort of bickering made me weary. They chattered like so many monkeys with orders, threats and dares. Nothing ever came of it. The watch changed or the bosun ordered them to shut up. My animal wariness could have taken a leave of absence for all the potential danger of this group.

I had been in an all-male society during the entire three months since leaving San Quentin. For the first six weeks I worked in a ship-yard and then, with Warden Duffy's recommendation, I had been able to enlist in the Merchant Marine. Now, I was on a Liberty ship that toiled slowly from Fremantle, Australia, to join a convoy at Columbo, Ceylon—if we were lucky.

Two nights before, as we were ready to pull out of Fremantle, a speech by President Roosevelt had been piped over the ship's public address system. In his memorable ringing tone, he recapitulated the history of America's fight for naval supremacy to protect the merchant shipping that was supplying our troops and our allies around the world. He said that the run from New York to Murmansk, once the most perilous, now was safe—thanks to the blanket of protection by our Navy ships and planes.

". . . and the lifelines have been secured by our naval forces to all of the free world except for the dangerous run from Fremantle, Australia, to Columbo, Ceylon. . . ." he added.

"Thanks a lot, Mr. President. That sure takes a load off our mind!" One man had voiced the thoughts of us all. The radio was shut down and we were on our way.

The warm, friendly darkness finally enveloped us after a tropical sunset that seemed to dally overlong. The plane was not there in the morning. Neither were any submarines, but no one felt easy until almost a week later, when we pulled into the harbor at Ceylon and dropped hook about a mile from the nearest merchant ship.

"Now, Coach?" someone yelled to the bosun, as the ship was secured. With his "Okay," about thirty men plunged into the harbor waters for a swim. This was standard procedure when an American ship arrived in these waters. On previous stops, I had been able to pick up a little money by betting that I could dive off the boat deck, the flying bridge or some promontory in the rigging. One day I collected $60 for a 60-foot dive, but I subsequently ran out of both promontories and takers. I only mention this because it had made me recognized on board our ship as a swimmer.

On this day I had plunged in and was content to let the cooling sea wash over my sweating body, as I swam close to the side of the ship. Before long, however, I noticed that every time some of the men scrambled up the Jacob's ladder in order to dive back in, a few remained on deck and pointed down to the clear water. Even while swimming, the sea was remarkably clear, but from the deck a man could see much further down, probably to a depth of fifty feet. In those depths lurked sharks, doubtless attracted by the refuse of the convoy.

This meant a halt might be called to our swimming. The heat was bad enough when we were underway, but at anchor here in the harbor, it was pitiless. The Navy gun crew assigned to our ship fired a few bursts from their .50-caliber machine guns in a line parallel to the ship, a few yards beyond where we were swimming. On the other ships, they were doing the same thing. It made swimming somewhat noisy.

"Okay, everybody out. Captain's orders!" The bosun's command had been predestined. Lingering, despite the danger of sharks, we stroked over to the Jacob's ladder, clambered aboard, grousing all the way.

We gathered mournfully on the fantail and cursed the long grey shapes darting beneath the surface. We were still in our trunks, but it was hard to tell when the sea water quit dripping and the perspiration began. The shark-warning flag was flying from the ship now, and a no-swimming broadcast had been beamed out from shore to the skippers.

Just then several pairs of eyes focused simultaneously on something in the water halfway between us and the next ship. We identified the object at the same time.

"Hey, there's someone out there."

A quick check of our crew revealed that the swimmer wasn't from our ship. Another quick check, through several pairs of binoculars, revealed something else—that he wasn't much of a swimmer. He was headed in our direction. With arms flailing and body bobbing he seemed to be making more progress up and down than forward. We surmised he had decided to swim from one ship to the other and had not heard the shark warning.

"I'll get the Captain's permission to lower a boat," the bosun said and was off to the flying bridge. Better hurry, I thought. It was obvious to me that sharks or no sharks, the man couldn't make it. Now almost every pair of eyes on ship was straining toward the swimmer, as if to support him until the boat reached him.

"No boat. I can't believe it." It was the bosun's breathless voice coming up behind us. "That's what the lunatic on the bridge told me—'No boat.' "

"Whaddya mean 'No boat'?" Several voices pounded indignantly. "Dincha tell 'im?"

"Of course, I told him. What the hell do you think? 'No boat will be lowered, is that clear?' he says. I says, 'Do you mean to tell me you're going to let an American sailor drown?' And he says, 'If he's that stupid, let the dumb son of a bitch drown.' Those are his exact words."

"Can't you put a boat down anyway?" I asked.

"Not against Captain's orders, I can't."

"Well, what are we gonna do, let him drown?"

The bosun didn't answer. He was a good man; he had been at sea before I was born. There was no sense in arguing with him, there was no time for arguing with the Captain. We had sometimes referred to him as "Captain Bligh" because of his disciplinary actions. But this was preposterous. Gradually, every eye had been turning in my direction. This was a fine time to be an authority on swimming.

It was a long dive from the fantail; long and wide, flattening at the end so I wouldn't go deep. In my anxiety I started off at a killing stroke that would have been fine in a 100-meter sprint, but I had a good quarter of a mile to go and back, if time—and the sharks—

would permit. I forced myself to a pace that could perhaps save us both.

The man lasted until I reached him. "I gotcha, man. I gotcha," I gasped. He didn't hear me. Fortunately, he was beyond getting me in a strangle hold. I pulled him to me, slung my left arm across his chest and gripped him by the right armpit. Then I started back. Head lolling, he trailed behind me, the water supporting most of his weight.

It was a lonesome return trip. And a long one, allowing plenty of time to be scared. All the time there was the threat of violence coiled beneath the surface—heavy, thick, oppressive. It penetrated every second of existence . . . the potential threat of sudden, ferocious annihilation.

A cheering section was above us as my right hand hit the Jacob's ladder. In one motion, I grabbed and tucked my feet to the lowest rung and remained there for a couple of seconds with my non-shark-proof butt still in the water. As a bosun's chair splashed beside me, I pulled the unconscious man's head and shoulders through it, draping him unceremoniously across it, belly down.

"Haul away," I yelled and scrambled up the Jacob's ladder with all of the agility of a rhesus monkey.

Strong hands helped me onto the deck, but I scarcely had the strength to stand up under the friendly slaps on the back and butt. I did, however, want to take a turn at artificial respiration on my prize from the sea, but there was no need. Under the ministrations of the men, great quantities of water had poured from his mouth, and now the sailor was beginning to choke and sputter.

"I've nothing but good news for you, Sewell," the bosun said by way of preamble. "Captain wants to see you, minute you come aboard."

"Like this?"

"Like that."

"Lead on, Bos."

The bosun led off to the flying bridge and I followed, still breathless and dripping. News of anything out of the ordinary is all over a ship in a matter of minutes, so by the time we arrived at the flying bridge quite a party had suddenly found some task to perform nearby.

The Captain was six feet tall and weighed about 140 pounds. His thin, deeply tanned and wrinkled face was livid.

"I understand you went in swimming after I ordered all men out of the water. Is that right?"

"Well, I didn't just go in for a swim, sir. I went in to . . ."

"Did you or did you not go into the water after I specifically ordered everyone out?"

"I did go in, sir, but it was an emergency. A man was drowning and . . ."

"And you knew it was against my orders when you went in, did you not?"

"I would not have gone in, sir, if the man could have made it alone. Or if you had lowered a boat."

"I am not in the habit of giving an explanation with my commands. I told the bosun and now I will tell you—if a man is so stupid that he doesn't know whether he can make the swim from one ship to another, then he deserves to drown. . . ."

I was weary to the point of exhaustion. I had been afraid—and to be afraid, no matter how reasonably, makes me angry. I refused to go on the defensive when I knew I was right.

"You'd let an American sailor drown when you had the power to save him? Well, I'm glad I got him, and I'd do it again. I've seen men locked up for ten years for less than . . . attempted murder."

"You can't talk to me like that." His voice was shrill.

"You old son of a bitch. I just got through talking to you like that," I pointed out. "I've heard that the captain is God on his ship. But you're not my God. Now just what the hell do you think you can do to scare me? That's been tried, Buster, by experts."

The Captain strode away, so I left. Down below in the crew's quarters I found the rescued sailor. Wrapped in a blanket, he was sitting on a bunk, drinking hot coffee, his lips still blue from shock. He stretched out a hand and tried to stand up when I came in. I sat down beside him and had coffee, too. In a matter of seconds the cabin filled with men. They had the latest from the bridge.

"Kay-rist, you should see old Bligh. He put out more orders about you in ten seconds than he's done during the whole damn war," one man volunteered.

"He's got you changed from the four-to-eight watch (the best working hours) to the eight-to-twelve (the worst)," said another.

A third man spoke up. "He's taking away all your overtime pay—what you've already earned."

I lay down on my own bunk. I had gone after the sailor at four o'clock; it was now almost six. The talk among the men continued at mess. I must have dropped off to sleep, for it was almost eight o'clock when the bosun entered.

"The Captain won't put a boat down to take the guy back to his ship. The kid's worried to death because when we all pull out for Calcutta in the morning, he'll be marked AWOL."

The bosun was a good man. He had again gone to the Captain with a plea for help. Permission had been denied. The Captain had even refused to signal the other ship so they would know what had happened and could send a boat for their man.

"The kid's going to try to swim it alone in a life jacket," the bosun said. "I can't let him do that, but I don't have the right to tell him not to."

"When I'm reincarnated, I hope it's as a dolphin," I said. Shortly after dark, the young sailor and I went quietly over the side and down the Jacob's ladder again with a small party of silent well-wishers to see us off.

This time the swim was much easier. The sailor was wearing a life jacket, and while I pushed him with what is called "the tired swimmer's carry," he helped by sculling and kicking as he lay on his back.

I had never thought of my size-11 feet as small. But as I looked at them kicking beneath the surface, they seemed like little morsels, especially tempting to large, hungry sharks. Every move we made cut a foamy, blue-green wake through the water. Under other circumstances it would have been beautiful, but I kept expecting rows of shivs to meet in my innards. Nothing would look beautiful to me right now except a deck under my feet. Sudden billows of phosphorescence breaking from time to time around us, denoting we were not alone in our starlit swim, were not reassuring either.

At last we were there. Another Jacob's ladder, another hull, strange faces on the deck watch. But they looked good to me.

Within a few minutes after we climbed onto the fantail deck, the sailor was summoned by his Captain. I remained in the crew's mess, drinking coffee and wearing borrowed dungarees, for about an hour before the Captain sent for me. I was braced for anything.

"Well, we're certainly in your debt, young man," he said and shook my hand. "My seaman has told me what you did. Your conduct is in keeping with the highest standards of the United States Maritime Service. Now, I'd like to ask you a few questions."

"Yes, sir."

"Is it true your Captain refused to lower a boat to rescue my man?"

"Yes, sir."

"How do you know he refused?"

"The bosun asked him when we first saw that your man couldn't make it. The bosun came back and told us that the Captain had refused to lower a boat. The Captain told me so, himself, later."

"What were his words to you?"

"He said he wasn't in the habit of explaining his orders, but he wasn't going to lower a boat because 'if the man is so stupid he doesn't know if he can make it from one ship to another, he deserves to drown.' "

"Were there any witnesses to this conversation?" The Captain, a stocky, wide-shouldered man, looked grim.

"I'll say there were—I mean, yes, sir."

I was put under examination, direct examination, cross examination and re-direct examination. Finally, the Captain said:

"Now, is there anything you have told me that you don't have personal knowledge of yourself?"

"He didn't actually tell me he was going to change my watch. Or that he was going to take all my back overtime pay. I just heard that. But the new watch list has been posted, and I have been changed, so I suppose he'll take my pay, too."

"Not by a damn sight, he won't. Now, pay attention to what I say. It is very important to you. When you get to Calcutta, go to the American Consul's office and prefer charges. I will go there and make a statement on your behalf and prefer charges of my own. Do you have that straight?"

"Yes, sir."

"Very well. Now, I will put down a boat to take you back to your ship. You understand there is a correct way of getting things done. I had to question you thoroughly and find out what was witnessed and what was not and exactly what was said. You understand that, don't you?"

"Yes, sir . . . and sir . . ."

"What is it?"

"Before you make any statement for me, perhaps you should know what I told the Captain." I then related my part of that notable conversation on the flying bridge, sparing none of the words I had used earlier. This Captain only smiled and said:

"That's fine. See you in Calcutta."

We arrived in Calcutta on schedule. But I was swung over the side in a stretcher, feet first. This was due to further ministrations of our beloved Captain Bligh. We were tying up at night at the Queen Ann docks on the Hooghli River when it happened. Through the megaphone from the bridge, the Captain's voice singled me out by name and ordered me to go forward for a heaving line. Since there were heaving lines all along the ship, it did not make sense for him to send me from one end to the other for one, especially in view of conditions on deck. Because of preparations for unloading a deck cargo of huge Black Widow night fighters, loose cables, braces, chocks, tools and other objects littered the available walking space. Previously, catwalks had spanned the planes, permitting the crew to move about the ship freely some eight or ten feet above the deck. Now, however, the catwalks were down. Only their supports, 6 x 6-inch beams, were still up—further impeding progress along the deck. It would have taken me a good ten minutes to make my way forward. "But if that's what the Captain wants I'd better get at it," I thought. As I started along the deck, the voice at the megaphone ordered:

"No. No. Get a move on, Sewell. Up on the supports and be quick about it."

Maybe he thought I would be scared. Scared enough to buck him over an order. One thing he didn't know was that my sense of balance was like a cat's. I'd show the old toad, I told myself, as I swung quickly to the top of the nearest beam. I made fast, erratic progress in 5-foot leaps from one beam end to the other. But finally, in the dark, I failed to see a steel cable that hung over the end of one beam. It rolled under my foot, and I hurtled downward. I managed to land on my feet, but the explosive "pop" I heard was the bone breaking in my left ankle. When I pulled my leg out from under me, I had a clear view of it—the bone was poking through the skin at a highly improbable angle.

There was a hazy pain-filled interlude of being lashed to a stretcher that swung out over the side of the ship in a cargo sling, of a ride in an Army ambulance, of a doctor who paid no attention to my ankle but rolled up one of my denim sleeves and mercifully sank a hypodermic needle into my arm.

Three days later they let me have visitors. I was sitting up in a hospital bed in a ward, surveying the huge cast on my leg. The pain had dulled. I could expect to be in the hospital for six weeks. The doctor told me bones knit slowly in the tropics. I wondered about my ship, about the American Consul and what was going to happen to me.

Who should be my first visitor? None other than our Captain Bligh. In he came, his hat in one hand, a sheaf of papers in the other.

"Well, now, Sewell, how are you, boy? Feeling better?" He smiled cordially, with a great show of solicitude.

The animal wariness within me was never at a higher peak. Mentally I circled him the way a belligerent dog circles another—stiff-legged, hackles up, shaken by inaudible growls, ripe for a fight to the death.

"I'll be okay," I said.

"The doctor says you'll be here a long time. We're going to have to sail without you." The Captain was trying to be chummy. "You can sign up on another ship, of course, as soon as you're well."

"This is no social call; what's on your conniving little mind?" my instincts kept shrieking. When a questioning cop suddenly becomes relaxed and sociable—beware!

"Well," he said heartily, "I wanted to see you, so I thought I might as well bring your discharge papers over myself. For you to sign."

So that was it. Since when did a skipper who had been told off as I had told him off come hat-in-hand to visit an ordinary seaman who was in the hospital because of the skipper's idiotic orders? Only when he needs something that seaman has.

"I'm not going to sign anything," I said.

"I don't understand. These are just your discharge papers. You always sign when you leave a ship."

"What else do you have there to sign?" That animal wariness could not be denied, although I knew his statement was accurate.

"Just a standard release form, absolving the shipping company from liability for your injury," he said, apparently encouraged because of my question. "Standard procedure; done all the time. You sign off and . . ."

"So that's it. You're the guy who said 'Let the son of a bitch drown.' Somehow I doubt that you'd have much compunction about letting another American sailor be stranded in India," I shouted. "Captain, you don't impress me. Where I came from the toughest man was also the kindest." Since he knew I had been in prison, and there are similarities in seagoing vernacular, I added, "Captain, where I came from, you'd have been turned out as a punk within fifteen minutes. You can stand there all day, but I won't sign a damn thing."

He didn't fume or sputter. He just remained standing with narrowed lids. Hatred gleamed in his eyes, then he wheeled and stalked out.

The swinging doors to the ward were still in motion from the Captain's exit when they burst inward again to admit a highly agitated seaman from my ship.

"You didn't sign anything, did you?" he exclaimed, pointing backward over his shoulder in the direction of the Captain's departure.

"I didn't sign anything."

"Hah! I told you he wouldn't. I knew he'd be too smart—didn't I tell you?" He addressed a passing nurse who had never laid eyes on either of us before.

"Settle down and give me the English translation," I suggested to my friend. He was the union representative of our ship.

"Well, I been busy, to put it mildly. But I'm not the only one." His dark eyes glowed with excitement. "Been to the American Consul. He told me to come here and tell you he'd be here himself, tomorrow.

"The skipper from the other ship paid the Consul a call in the middle of the night. Right after we docked—didn't even wait till morning, they say. Boy, he was hotter than a pistol about our Captain saying 'Let the guy drown.' He musta really told the Consul.

"Man, things got busy around there. The Consul got sworn statements from half the guys on our ship, from this other Captain and from the guy you pulled out. Anyway, he says for you to sit tight till tomorrow."

"Okay, I won't go anyplace," I said ironically. But I was touched. Here was a man I scarcely knew, yet he had spent his entire liberty working unselfishly on my behalf. There was nothing in it for him. The spirit that had inspired him brought one of my more nebulous concepts into focus.

The American Consul paid me a visit the following day. Tall, tanned, grey at the temples and immaculately clad in a tropical white suit, he was the image of a successful executive. That he was also an efficient one became clear at once.

"Everything is in order so you will keep all previously accrued monies due you, receive full pay while hospitalized and get your expenses back to the port of San Francisco or until you sign onto another ship. These monies will be sent directly to the American Consulate, where you can draw all or part at any time you wish. Everything will be released to you when you leave Calcutta."

He had been drawing papers out of a briefcase, one by one, explaining each. "I am going to inform you of your rights," he said. "The Captain's order to have you run along the catwalk supports was in direct violation of United States Maritime safety regulations. I think it behooves you to consult an attorney on your return to the States. He can inform you whether you have cause for action. My offhand opinion is that you do."

He put all of the affidavits and papers back into his briefcase— except one that he picked up and handed to me.

"I'm sure you will understand this without any explanation," he said. I picked up the sheet he had left and read:

"For heroism beyond the line of duty . . ."

It was a commendation for the leap into the bay at Ceylon that had plunged me into this mess. I looked at it, looked inward and wondered.

That the Captain would allow a man to drown didn't shock me particularly. Nor did the fact that I would go to his rescue. It was something that had to be coped with at the time. In reform school and in my early days in prison, authority had been brutal, punishing. Therefore, the continuation of it "outside" didn't bother me too much. It wasn't until years later that it dawned on me that the Captain of my ship had been the wild exception to the rule.

There is something about a hospital siege that makes you go within yourself, to explore the hidden little caves of the subconscious where old incidents are stowed. Why they come to the surface of your mind at this particular time may puzzle you, but in the total picture of your life, they do have significance. The last time I had been in a hospital was to visit my friend, Red. Red who was there because he saved my life in the yard of San Quentin. That was when I was taking the first steps toward becoming a whole person. Perhaps I thought of him for two reasons. He had said in his wry manner that my contribution toward Warden Duffy's program was doing good. And later, in my own way, I had been able to repay his selfless act toward me.

It happened after I was out of San Quentin and working on the docks. One evening, as I got off my job, I noticed a semi-circle of men, angry and threatening, ringed around something. Over their heads, some twenty feet away, was the focal point of their anger. It was Red. He was backed up on the platform of a warehouse, against the wall, and he was holding a longshoreman's hook in each hand. He was daring them to advance.

I pushed through the crowd, drawing my own hook from my belt. Red recognized me.

"Boy, am I glad to see you," he exclaimed, showing no surprise at my presence. His voice had a ring to it as he shouted at the men, "Okay, this makes it even—two against twenty." With that, he plunged forward confidently. I covered his back. The men dispersed; we were left alone. His belligerence evaporated. We laughed, belted our hooks and shook hands. Red said he had been released a few weeks earlier; he had taken the job on the waterfront only to satisfy his parole officer. "I got bigger fish to fry," he announced jauntily.

He wanted to buy me a drink, naturally, but when I declined on the grounds that it would violate the terms of my parole, he commented sadly that it looked to him as if I wouldn't be interested in his big plans.

"Got a heist lined up," he confided genially. "Should be worth sixteen grand if it's worth a penny. Naw—" he waved off my interruption. "I know you, Bill. You gave your word to Duffy an' I know you'll keep it. But me, I'm different.

"I'm impatient, kid. I'm restless. Workin' like hell, eight, ten hours a day, punchin' a time clock, waitin' a week for a ratty little paycheck that don't do more than buy groceries—that ain't my idea of how to live. I got a good wife; she's so solid and she deserves better'n a longshoreman's pay."

Nothing I could say out of my own experience would appeal to his way of thinking. My crime sprees had never been prompted by need. The press called my type of criminal a "thrill bandit."

Well, I'd had all the thrills I wanted that way. So Red and I parted, warmly but for good, I thought. However, a week later, I heard from him again—indirectly, this time.

It was five o'clock in the morning when my disgruntled landlord called me to the hall telephone of the rooming house where I was living.

"Is this Bill?" a woman's voice asked. "Bill Sewell, 66836?"

To hear my prison number again brushed all sleep from my brain. "Yes," I replied. "Who is this?"

"Red's wife." She repeated his prison number. "He said I could call you if I ever needed help."

"Sure. What's wrong?"

"He isn't home yet." She paused. "Bill, have you heard the radio newscast this morning?"

"Not yet."

"Well, he's on it. He's out somewhere in Hollywood. That's where he went last night, and they've got him surrounded. The guy with him got winged, but he made it back here. But Red must be hiding out someplace."

It was six o'clock when I got to Red's apartment. The first morning papers were on the stands. The front pages carried a story of a running gunfight the previous night between the police and two bandits. The bandits had abandoned their bullet-punctured car on a Hollywood side street and had fled on foot. Police had the street blocked off and were making a minute search of the area.

In the apartment, I found Red's wife, a pleasant, attractive, but thoroughly frightened woman and his partner, who was suffering from a superficial wound on his wrist. He had managed to elude the police by dodging into an all-night movie. He brought with him the money from the stickup.

"Take me back there," I suggested to him, "and show me where you guys left the car."

"Are you out of your mind?" he shouted. He was paralyzed by fright, and the wound did immobilize him. He was no help to me. Besides the newspapers told me enough. I started out in Red's own car—he had used a stolen one for the robbery—and his wife insisted on coming with me.

You're just asking for trouble, I told myself grimly, as we sped from San Pedro to Hollywood. Known as a former prison associate of Red's, here I was in Red's car with Red's wife. I was an ex-convict with forty-seven years ahead of me if I were apprehended in the area where the police were searching for Red. Officers would certainly be satisfied that I had been his partner in crime the previous night. And what jury would believe me innocent?

I thought of Warden Duffy.

I thought of Red.

"This is sure swell of you," said Red's wife.

"Red saved my life," I told her, and to myself, I added, *and if it had not been for Warden Duffy, it would not have been worth saving or living. How can I let down either of them?*

"Let me out here," I said to Red's wife when we reached the area where the stolen car had been abandoned. I walked the length of the next two blocks in one direction. I was whistling and singing softly the theme song of "San Quentin on the Air," interspersing the notes of "Time on my Hands" with "red ones, red ones." On I walked, up one side of the street, down the other, two blocks to my left, two to my right, until I had completely circled the area.

Police were much in evidence. Black-and-white cars were cruising the area, and both uniformed and plainclothesmen were on foot. After almost an hour of circling various blocks, I finally came to a street where skid marks and broken glass showed where the auto-mobile chase had ended. A chunk of plaster was missing from a stucco house on the corner; marks of bullet holes pitted the adjacent wooden fence. I slowed my pace but continued my song.

A sound came from the nearby shrubbery. "Pssst."

There was Red. He must have been crouching in the thick hedge all night. I dared not look around, but I bent down and pretended to tie my shoe, all the while singing softly. The tune was the same but the words were different. The new lyrics told him I would go away and return with the car, and that the rear door would be open.

And that's what I did. We drove slowly down the street. I was at the wheel in case a chase developed; Red's wife was in the front seat beside me, holding onto the handle of the rear door. No one was in sight as I slowed almost to a stop beside those skid marks. Suddenly the shrubbery exploded, and Red's stocky form arced in a dive that landed him facedown in the back of the car. His wife pulled the door shut. We resumed our slow drive.

When we were once more in his apartment, Red laughed. "Man, that was sure close. We run right into this damn stakeout just as I'm pullin' away. Now they tell me. . . ." He waved grandly at the newspaper. ". . . this place has been bothered coupla times lately, so the cops were there. But the big dough wasn't."

The sack of loot amounted to some $1,600, instead of the anticipated $16,000.

"Bill, you take it all. I'll look after my partner here." Red shoved the money sack toward me as his partner nodded assent. I could only shake my head in refusal. All the time I was walking and whistling, I was praying, too. *If You'll just get me out of this one, so I don't let down Warden Duffy . . . if You can't get me out of it, I'd rather have the cops kill me right here. . . .*

I knew that if I touched any of that money, I would be taken back to San Quentin. Knew it as I had known that time in the county jail that my father would not be able to get me out of prison.

I was going one way, and Red was going another. And we both knew it.

We shook hands.

"All accounts squared?" I asked.

"Square," he said with a grin.

Six weeks later, Red was gunned to death in a street fight with the San Francisco police.

Shortly after my encounter with Red, I had another significant meeting, a constructive one that was to influence me for the rest of my life. It began one morning when I was having breakfast in the vast waterfront cafeteria called Wilmington Hall, which was frequented by shipyard workers, longshoremen and others who made up the bulk of waterfront society. Across the table from me sat an individual whom I had seen in the shipyards. "Hardway" was the only name I knew for him; it stemmed from his gambling in a floating crap game. It was rumored that he lost his paycheck and more each week. This was the first time I had seen him at close hand, and the toughness of the man surprised me. He must have been fifty years old. He stood taller than my six feet, two inches, and his shoulders practically blotted out the horizon. But it was his expression that warned you that this was no man to tangle with. His eyes were cold and blue as cobalt, and there was an iron set to his jaw.

Suddenly, a stranger was at our table, addressing himself to the man opposite me.

"I think I'll make you move, old man."

Looking up, I recognized a bully boy I had seen here on several previous mornings. It was this ogre's custom to choose a table already occupied by several men and drive them off with threats. Empty tables didn't appeal to him; there was no opportunity for him to show off. I was still doing my own time so, until he decided to single me out, I ignored him. But that morning, he chose the wrong man.

"Hardway" glanced up at the bully, then continued calmly eating. He said without ire, "You're not so tough."

"Who says I ain't tough, you old son of a bitch?"

"I do." "Hardway" put down his knife and fork but made no move to rise. Instead of looking directly into the face of his tormentor, the older man was eyeing the other's muscular thighs, where they pressed against the edge of the table. Then, with a swift gesture, he whipped his hand along the table surface toward the bully's legs and rapped him hard—squarely between them.

The man went down. His food tray went up. No one else had seen what happened; it was too fast. What they did see was a large man, lying in the foetal position on the floor, rolling, moaning gibberish, his lips foaming in agony.

To the frantic manager's queries of "What happened?" there was no answer from anyone, until "Hardway" finally offered:

"I think he's having a fit."

And I had a difficult time containing my mirth as police and ambulance were summoned, and the erstwhile bully, still unable to utter a coherent word, was hauled off in a straitjacket.

Later that day, I again saw "Hardway." At the end of my shift I was wearily putting aside the 16-pound sledge when he walked by. Thinking himself unobserved, he was folding some bills onto a roll of money so thick his huge hand could scarcely fit around it. *His luck must have changed*, I thought. He looked up, saw me, and a smile warmed his face.

"Don't believe everything you hear about old 'Hardway's' luck," he remarked. "You're the only one who's ever seen this roll. But it's all right. You'll keep your mouth shut."

"As a matter of fact, I will," was my reply, "but how did you know you could trust me?"

"I know what kind of man you are," he said with a quiet smile, "and where you've been."

"What the hell d'you mean, 'Where I've been'?" No one on the waterfront knew about my past.

"Take it easy; no one tipped me off," he said. "I just know, that's all. I can see right into people."

I was angry and puzzled. Whatever was he talking about?

"It's just a feeling I get about some people and some situations." He was at a loss to explain what turned out to be a phenomenal psychic faculty.

"Take yourself, for instance," he continued. "You were probably an only child, lots of money, ambitious parents. It isn't that you were spoiled. It's hard to tell exactly what the trouble was. Anyway, it was the demon on your back. You've been driven to prove you're tough. You were always hitting back. 'I'll show 'em,' you said to yourself.

"Then it probably caught up with you. Prison?" He didn't wait for my answer. "Most men in prison get worse. You got better. You learned most of the lessons a man must learn in order to be happy. You had to learn them in order to survive. Right?"

"How the hell do you know this?"

He shrugged momentarily, the blue eyes softened. "I don't know. I call it 'the angel on my shoulder.' I've been a rounder all my life, but I never spent a night in jail. My angel warns me whom to stay away from and what places to avoid. I don't exactly know what it is, but I've learned to listen to it."

That encounter led to a warm and remarkable friendship that has endured through the years and is one of the precious tokens of my life.

It was through "Hardway"—whose name, I learned, was Jim—that I was able, at last, to evaluate my mother's character and her place in my life.

I saw her not as a symbol of the saintly security in life that a child sees and that makes him so vulnerable to her very human traits of anger, displeasure or frustration. I learned to accept her as another human being, neither enemy nor friend. I knew then, and so it developed, that I would see her again over the years, but with no emotional involvements and certainly never again with heartbreak.

As for my father, my new insight confirmed the good feelings that were no longer immobilized within me. He had tried valiantly in the brief span of our time together to make up for my deprivations, and he had done it in generous terms—a new car, a wardrobe from his own tailor, an introduction to every important headwaiter in town, even the right to his own checking account. That his bounty had a deleterious effect on me was not his fault. He had tried so hard to do what was right according to his concepts. He had even asked me to write my mother regularly, and in his courteous, thoughtful way, stressed my obligations to her.

I welcomed the clothes, the car, the open checking account for what they were worth to a kid. Especially because my mother had kept me on an allowance of 25 cents a week for spending money, when most boys of 16 in similar circumstances, were receiving fifty times as much.

But my mother's peculiar need to inflict hurt and my father's terrible need to compensate for a sin of which he wasn't guilty had both been too much for a boy of my emotional caliber.

Only now did I begin to understand. I didn't hate my mother anymore. I was indifferent when I thought of her. I learned that hatred isn't the opposite of love.

The opposite of love is indifference.

I also told Jim about the episode with Red. He merely nodded. "Quit throwing rocks at the front gate of San Quentin," he advised.

A few nights later, Jim and I were walking down the street after work and I swung into a bar for a pack of cigarettes. Jim waited outside. As the bartender handed me the pack from behind the bar and I reached to pay him, one of us must have accidentally jostled a large, curly-haired man on a barstool. He turned on me in a fury.

"What the hell's the big idea? Look what you're doin'."

Instinctively, I set myself for him, but remembering San Quentin, held myself in check. My hesitation was clearly interpreted as cowardice. He grabbed me by the jacket. "Don't you like it? What the hell d'you intend doin'?"

Invective flowed forth, engulfing me and silencing the bar. The toughest discipline was to keep quiet, to remind myself I was on parole and couldn't be caught in a bar even though I, myself, was not drinking. Fighting by parolees, unless in unmistakable self-defense, is considered assault. This was another peril. If this went much farther, it could land me back in San Quentin facing Warden Duffy.

It took all of my self-control, but I did manage to back out of the door amid laughter from the other patrons and farewell insults from my tormentor.

Outside, Jim was waiting up the street. One look at me told him something was amiss. I couldn't speak for a few minutes, but finally the tide of fury poured out. I thrust the cigarettes in his hand and turned back.

"Jim, I can't stand it. No one can talk to me like that and get away with it. I could whip him and a couple more like him. I can't let him sit and sneer, thinking he had me scared. I just can't. . . ."

I felt the incredible power of Jim's arms as he grabbed me and hung on. By sheer physical strength, he prevented my getting away.

"Who do you have to prove you're tough to?" he demanded savagely. "Me? I already know it. Yourself? You know it, too. Hell, if you know it, what d'you care whether some stranger does or not? You going to risk forty-seven years of time just for the satisfaction of breaking in that idiot's face? You going to let down the Warden and his wife for one lousy display of temper?

"If that's all you've learned, Bill, then you aren't the man I thought you were."

He dropped his hands. I took a step toward the bar, swung around and faced him again. His pale blue eyes seemed charged with electricity.

"Don't worry about that hoodlum," he said more quietly. "He'll get his. He can't escape it. A man doesn't go through life doing that to people without getting busted in turn. We all get what's coming to us, right here in this life. Heaven or hell, it's of our own making."

After I had simmered down, he invited me to his house for dinner, and there I met his wife for the first time. I had thought of him as the world's toughest man and now it seemed to me she was the world's sweetest woman. She moved with the grace of a professional dancer, and it turned out that she had been one. To my surprise, they lived in a suite at the Santa Monica Biltmore. Most of the men at the shipyard thought of "Hardway" as a compulsive gambler, broke most of the time. The truth was that he was a professional, and although he knew every trick of the trade, he was scrupulously honest. As a matter of fact, he was a member in good standing of several local exclusive men's clubs, where he played poker. He was frequently hired by other establishments to keep the game on the square by detecting cheats.

One of the funniest experiences in his life occurred when a couple of men at the shipyard had introduced crooked dice in a crap game. "I could hear 'em gallop," Jim said wryly. But he had lost his money, along with the others. That night, he came home and from a dresser drawer that lodged hundreds of pairs of dice, he selected a pair that exactly matched the "gallopers" used in the shipyard game. Jim's dice, however, were honest.

He went back to the crap game the following day. He palmed the crooked dice, tossed back his own and cleaned house while the two lame-brains in charge of the old dice kept making wrong bets, each time plunging deeper into debt.

"They beat me till they were broke," Jim said with a chuckle.

It took a good deal of persuasion on Jim's part to make me dismiss from my mind the incident of the bully in the bar. Several times I was tempted to go back and find him. But Jim's wisdom had done its work against my will. A week later we were having breakfast at Wilmington Hall when Jim exclaimed, "Speaking of beatings, there goes a guy as bad off as any I've ever seen on his feet."

I followed his gaze and saw a horrible apparition. What had probably been a well-set-up man came shuffling in. He was stooped and leaned on a cane with one hand; the other was in a sling. He wore a "turban," and his face was mottled to the color of ripe plums. His eyes were swollen, one of them shut. Great lines of unbandaged stitches showed across his nose, on his cheekbones and at the corners of his mouth. He was indeed a hideous and pitiful sight.

Suddenly I recognized him by the curly hair hanging from under the head bandage. I stood up to look into his eyes as he shuffled by, but I intended him no harm.

"You're the tough guy," I said.

"I ain't tough, mister," he said with a quaver, trying to locate me with a half-open eye. There was no recognition in his look. "I ain't tough—I'm sick—bad. . . ."

I sat down, deep in thought. My experience with Red had shaken me up wildly. It had caused me to pray. But it had not implanted knowledge, firsthand shattering knowledge. I looked at Jim across the table from me. I thought of the unbelievable strength he had used to hold me back several days ago. I saw his pleasant, relaxed smile. His wife had told me he would go miles out of his way to stay out of a beef. Yet he could, without exaggeration, probably kill any belligerent who ever confronted him. When I spoke, I knew it was with enduring truth.

"I'll never go back to prison, I know it. Now, I know it."

"Bill," Jim said quietly, "whatever a man's mind can conceive, a man can achieve. I know you won't go back. You'll learn the hard way. But you won't go back."

There should be a Big Jim in every young man's life. Someone who has faced truths and has the heartwarming skill to impart them to others. Someone who is calm and wise and tough with the true toughness of inner strength. Whenever I reflected on my first days out of prison, I thanked God mentally for Warden Duffy. And now I thanked Jim just for being alive.

As I lay in the hospital thinking of the Duffy's and of Jim, I began to perk up and I wrote to them and tried to tell them what they meant to me. First I had no parents, now I seemed to have two sets.

Two weeks later my ship, the S. S. *Oliver Wendell Holmes*, sailed away from Calcutta. My shipmates, however, left me well fixed. Our union representative told me he had already written to a California firm of attorneys who would be glad to handle my case. They would get full documentation from the files of the United States Consular offices in Calcutta and from the log of our ship. They followed through. Eventually, I accepted a settlement of $3,600 in damages. The Captain, incidentally, was later stripped of his command over other misconduct at a hearing I didn't even have to attend.

A month after the ship sailed, a final cast was fitted to my ankle, and I was pronounced ready for release. My prolonged hospital stay had been made bearable by the book cart that was rolled to our beds by the courtesy of the American Red Cross. The Red Cross girl who pushed it was shapely and highly intelligent. She possessed other attributes, as I was to discover.

That was how Karen came into my life. Since my release from San Quentin, I had scarcely seen a woman. In San Pedro, I had worked in the shipyards and at the end of the day was usually so beat that I hit my hotel-room bed and slept until morning.

Then it was the Merchant Marine. In Fremantle, Australia, there had been trouble between American sailors and Australian servicemen before our arrival. As a result, we were kept aboard the ship during our brief stopover. But I was about to change my celibate status, I told myself.

When I told her I was a civilian and that I had a few bucks in my kick, Karen became really interested. Not in the bucks, but in the fact that my civilian status would give me complete freedom when I was released from the hospital. We made a dinner date for my first evening. I took her to Firpo's Restaurant. In the massive 2-story dining room lighted only by table lamps, red-silk-pantalooned waiters moved barefoot on the thick oriental pile, their white turbans like moons in the incense-laden darkness. We partook of one exotic food after another, and we drank liberally of the Firpo specialty, a potent fruit punch.

She was only mildly interested in my family background. It was my stay in San Quentin that fascinated her.

"What did you do about sex in prison?" she asked.

"I did without. What else?"

"Well, I've heard so many stories. That when a man goes to prison, he must make up his mind, at the very beginning, whether he is going to be male or female."

"You heard it all wrong," I replied. That was perhaps when I first realized that most people have no idea of what is going on in their prisons. "In prison, there are some sex deviates. They've usually been committed for sex crimes. But they are segregated by the rest of the men, who have no use for them. They are branded 'rapos,' and their lives are made exceedingly difficult.

"Strangely enough, Mexico and most Latin countries solve the problem of the normal prisoner's sex drive with greater intelligence than we do. There's this thing of conjugal visits—wives come to see their husbands in prison. My own opinion is that sex deviates should be segregated for the good of others. You take a bank robber and a sex deviate—they're both law breakers. But their characters are almost diametrical opposites. Robbery is something you do. Rapist is something you are."

My answers seemed satisfactory to her. I found myself liking this girl. She had sensitivity as well as intelligence. But no matter what subject we started on, it seemed to lead to a discussion of sex.

I told her of my boyish adventures in the Hawaiian Islands. But even as we were talking, I realized that regardless of what had happened to me before, I was heading for my first sex adventure as an adult male. It wasn't long before I was up on my crutches, paying the check and then helping her into a rickshaw in the heat-filled dark of the street. We went to the Great Eastern Hotel, where I had taken a room. My first move earlier had been to prepare it for just such an occasion. I had changed the white light bulbs to softly colored ones, had ordered whiskey and ice to be served at a later hour. Now, as we walked in from the interior balcony, the room was inviting, and the liquor was waiting on a low table by the oriental couch. My cast and crutches were somewhat of a handicap, but I managed to pour a couple of drinks. Karen took it from there. We started at midnight. By morning we had drained both the whiskey and our passions. Karen got up, dressed and went to work. I lay exhausted in bed.

This was the beginning of an erotic binge that lasted for ten days. Karen was almost insatiable—almost, but not quite. Each morning she would leave for her job at the hospital and I would remain supine, like a mortally wounded man. In Karen, the need for love was voracious. It seemed to me that no man could satisfy her and live to remember his experiences. After two years of celibacy, I had a lot to make up for in this department, but when the eleventh morning dawned, I decided I had made up sufficiently for at least a 5-year stretch. I wrote Karen a note and left it at the hotel desk. Then I went to the American Consul's office and asked if I could finish my recuperation leave in Bombay. I checked out my money and possessions and bought a train ticket to the other end of India.

After a long and satisfying sleep, I began to enjoy myself. I was traveling first class, which entitled me to check out a clean, fumigated sleeping bag and to have the exclusive use of a wooden bench to spread it on. I bought several large clay jugs of purified water and took enough sandwiches to last most of the trip.

Under normal circumstances, a journey through the interior of India would have been fascinating. But my ankle still hurt. I was near exhaustion, therefore what the trip actually represented for me was an opportunity to rest and think.

The concepts on love that I had formed at San Quentin were the results of taking on faith the teachings of Plato and others (along with some of my own wishful thinking) that sex was not in itself an end.

I had solved Karen's problem for the moment, but I had also solved one of my own. Because Karen had served to reinforce the knowledge I had been taking on faith alone. That there was more to love than the physical act. That sex was not an emotion in itself, but the means of conveying the deepest, the greatest, existing emotion. It was not an end, but a means to an end. That so far my experience had been nothing more than an act of sex. That I had nothing to convey, no love, no mutual respect, no mental compatibility. There had to be someone, somewhere, who could inspire that response within me. I resolved that somehow, some day, I would find her.

The train was slowing again. Here was Bombay. I looked out the window at the unbelievably crowded streets, where hordes of people in saris and soiled white garments mingled with men in uniforms of the Allied armies of the world. Nearby was a huge burning ghat with its mourners, the size of the funeral pyre denoting the wealth and importance of the deceased Hindu. A young mahout guided an elephant through the crowds where bicycles, jeeps and rickshaws drove slowly but perilously through the incredible press of foot traffic.

On a nearby hill was what appeared to be a great circular fort of grey stone, four or five stories high, its circumference embracing the area of a city block. Above it the sky was black with huge birds that scarcely moved their wings, seeming to float in endless circles.

"That is the Tower of Silence," said a voice at my shoulder. Turning, I saw a well-dressed Hindu who had spent most of the trip reading English medical journals. In addition to his sleeping roll, he carried a physician's standard black bag. He now introduced himself as a doctor and asked if this were my first time in India.

"The Tower of Silence is where the Parsees dispose of their dead," he explained. "The building is completely hollow. It consists merely of the outside walls that you see. The top is open; there is no roof. On each level is a ring of metal doors that can be opened so that a body may be set inside on a grate. After the bodies are picked clean, the bones drop through the grating down to the bottom of the interior. The grates are seldom empty," he explained matter-of-factly. I wanted to ask what it was that picked the bones of the dead, but I looked up at the host of birds and remained silent.

Everywhere in India, in the midst of life there is death—in public cremation, in this tower, in the turgid rivers. What a turnover of human life, I thought. A never-ending race between birth and death.

"Come, my young friend," said the doctor in his Oxford English.

"The cycle of life and death is always with us. But meanwhile, many strange and exotic sights are to be enjoyed. Here is my card. I would like you to join me at my club tomorrow. For rest, shall we say, and conversation?"

7

I ACCEPTED THE DOCTOR'S GRACIOUS INVITA-
tion and later joined his club, The Bombay Cricket Club of India. The swimming
pool was an extra inducement; once the
cast was removed, water exercise would
help me regain the use of my ankle. Meanwhile, I enjoyed the sun and the company.

During my first visit I noticed a little
Indian girl of about 12 taking a competition swimming workout with her coach,
who was, it developed, her father. After
he heard I had qualified for the United
States Olympic water polo team in 1940,
he invited my comments on his daughter's
progress. With the directness that has

often been my undoing, I took him literally. I suggested she had a long way to go before she could be considered serious competition.

He was startled and indignant. He announced curtly that I was looking at the champion woman swimmer of India. And he·was telling the truth.

He was realistic, however, and after his momentary chagrin, suggested that perhaps I could achieve better results. Here, the inner discipline I had acquired at San Quentin proved helpful to both of us. I initiated a program of coaching; she took direction with enthusiasm and within a week showed marked improvement in form and against the stopwatch. A short time later, the coach of the male swim team asked me to visit his training sessions. The Indian swimmers were competent. What they lacked was the aggressive, all-out drive that is characteristic of American athletes. But they were willing and good sports; they needed only to be shown. Shortly afterward, the Bombay officials of the All-India Olympics—they were holding their own games in 1944, since most nations were at war—asked me to take on the job of head coach. This was a project that appealed to me. I had always been competitive, and at this period of my life, I needed to go all out for a project. Finally, three months after my injury, the cast was removed from my ankle. Until then, my swimmers had taken me on faith; now it was time for me to prove myself in the water. It took weeks to get my withered leg back in action, but I did manage to satisfy the crew as to my ability. The Bombay swimming teams, both men and women, went on to the games in Calcutta, swept away all competition and brought home all trophies.

I was restless, however. I had become acquainted with American soldiers and sailors on leave from military hospitals. But gradually, one by one, they disappeared from the scene, either shipping out or going stateside. When I could walk without a cane, I reported to the American consulate to inquire about a ship. But all of our vessels had full crews, and I was obliged to return to the United States on a hospital ship, the *General A. E. Anderson.*

Within a week after my arrival in San Francisco I had signed aboard another vessel. It was hot in Manila that summer. The invading Americans hadn't yet retaken all of the Philippines. The rumble of gunfire could be heard to the north of us and out at sea. We were then part of a line of convoys that stretched from horizon to horizon, all American shipping. Although this run was much less perilous than my earlier trips, I didn't realize the closing days of war were approaching as we pulled into Manila harbor.

In the hideously damaged city, I found a gymnasium that was untouched. I paid a visit there one afternoon and for a small fee was allowed to work out. As I tried to regain my former timing on the light striking bag, a well-dressed Filipino came over to watch me.

"Have you ever fought?" he asked.

"Some."

"My name is Rafael Apeng Reyes. I am matchmaker for Manila Square Gardens. If you are going to be here for a while, perhaps I could make you some money as a main-eventer."

That's how it began—one of the world's shortest careers as a professional prize fighter. Weighing 185 pounds, I was matched against everything from middleweights through heavyweights. Unfortunately, I won all my bouts, mostly three-rounders, and mostly by knockouts. Then, as K. O. Billy Sewell, I fell victim to delusions of grandeur. It was my idea to ask for a bout with Art Acosta, a real pro light heavyweight. The match was arranged. I launched an intensive two-week training program. The night of the fight was to me Madison Square Garden. Art Acosta, dancing in the opposite corner, might have been Joe Louis.

And well he might. Acosta was clearly unimpressed by my flurry of leather; he caught everything on his gloves and forearms that I had to give. Suddenly, I realized I was sitting down—my opponent was skipping away from me to a far corner. Overhead, the bright lights were dancing.

". . . three, four . . ."

The referee was counting me out! I managed to get up, pushed him aside and rushed at Acosta. The referee caught me and wiped my gloves against his shirt while he peered into my eyes. Then he let me go, which was a mistake on his part and mine. There were then no mandatory eight-counts or three-knockdown rules. I was knocked down in every round, six times in the final round.

That was the end of my career as a boxer.

Shortly after that all the fighting was over. Our ship was on the way back to the United States when the Bomb was dropped. When the excited crew disembarked at San Francisco, I became one of millions of young men about to start on an uncertain future. In spite of the deep inner drives to make something of myself, the goal ahead was unclear. That it should involve physical action and excitement, however, seemed certain, for I was full of healthy male-animal drive.

At least I'm not without money, I thought, at the end of the war. Since childhood, I had known that at the age of 25 I would come into a trust fund of $25,000 that had been left to me by my father's parents. When I showed up at the Los Angeles bank, where it was being held until after my birthday, the manager had some news for me. All that was left of the fund was about $3,000.

"Your mother drew out the rest for your education," he explained after checking a sheaf of papers. And all the time, I had thought the State of California had footed the bill for my education. For it was only in San Quentin that I had learned how to learn.

I put what was left of the trust to good use. In a "Business Opportunities" ad, I read of a taxicab company for sale. Its assets were two 6-year-old limousines in good condition and a tiny office. The owner had an exclusive franchise to service a small resort hotel located near Camp Pendleton, the enormous Marine Corps station. Business was brisk on weekends as thousands of servicemen took off to spend liberty in Los Angeles. I bought half the company; an ex-Marine friend came in for the other half. My parole officer was well pleased with the fact that I had my own business. In fact, my parole was discharged shortly thereafter.

After several months of being entirely free, I decided it was time to move—and keep moving. I sold out my share and moved to Lake Arrowhead in the San Bernardino mountains. There I formed another cab company. But business was so bad that I took a construction job to supplement my earnings.

I developed into a fair carpenter, a competent electrician and the world's worst plumber. I can climb poles, string wire, unravel electrical mysteries. But put me with any kind of pipe, and I'll show you a disaster looking for a place to happen. I did, however, construct a snug cabin for myself to live in. My construction job was for the County of San Bernardino. Two months later, the county superintendent gave notice of his resignation and, to my surprise, submitted my name as his replacement.

"All you need to do now is to make out the budget for the coming fiscal year," he said. "Take it to the county board of supervisors, pray they give you what you need—and that's it."

Again a new challenge. I made a painstaking study of our equipment, checked cost and location of the least expensive replacements for old machinery, figured what I needed in the way of additional supplies, estimated everything, and then, finally, readied a full report for the supervisors' annual budget hearing.

I waited nervously while the 5-man board studied it, point by point. After what seemed hours, the chairman sat back, took off his glasses and smiled.

"Do you realize the budget you have submitted is some $20,000 under any we have received in recent years?" He went on: "We will be very happy if you can keep the expenditures in your district within what you have outlined. You may consider the job yours."

"Thank you," I said gravely. And then added what had to be said.

"Gentlemen, if you decide to change your minds about my having this position after you've heard what I have to say, there'll be no hard feelings on my part. But you are entitled to know that in 1941 I pleaded guilty to committing a felony, and that I served two years and three months in San Quentin Prison. I was paroled in 1943 and have had no similar actions, convictions or sentences." I added, "You are welcome to check with San Quentin's warden, Mr. Clinton T. Duffy, about my record, my character, the circumstances of my parole and anything else you may wish to ask. Meanwhile I assure you I can stay within the budget I have outlined, and I know I can handle the work crews to your satisfaction."

The five men looked at each other, at me, and then, out the window. Then the chairman said, "That's fine. We appreciate the information. Is there anything further?"

"No, sir."

"Well, then, suppose you get back to the mountains and start concentrating on this work."

He had placed his faith in me. At the end of the year, I not only stayed within the budget but made additional purchases and came out with a surplus to boot.

It was a wonderful job, and Lake Arrowhead was a wonderful place to live. There were year-round sports—hunting, fishing, horseback riding, hiking, swimming, water skiing and snow skiing, and I participated in all of them. Many men, I am sure, would have been happy there for life.

But not I. I had decided to taste and savor and digest every morsel of life that I could lay my hands on. A year and a half later, I applied for a job as a construction clerk with the Arabian American Oil Company (Aramco). My references were checked; among them was the strong recommendation of the chairman of the San Bernardino Board of Supervisors. I was hired in spite of my criminal record.

I flew to New York, and then, with several other new employees, was flown to Dhahran, Arabia in one of the oil company's Constellation planes. On the last leg we winged out over the indigo of the Mediterranean, then across the endless sand dunes of Arabia itself. At last, was Dhahran, our future home. Rising out of the sands below was a modern community of new homes on curving streets and a business section of well-spaced concrete-and-steel office buildings. Soon we were rolling down the runway of a nearby United States Army Air Force Base.

"Take a deep breath," the smiling stewardess instructed as she took up a position by the plane door.

The door opened. We were momentarily stunned. The heat that billowed through that plane doorway hit us like a sledge-hammer. The official temperature in Dhahran that afternoon was 133 degrees.

Coats and neckties came off immediately. But we were all soaked with perspiration by the time we were taken by bus to the modern Aramco-built community. The houses we had seen from the air were spacious, attractive and rent-free to men with families. Each house boasted a startlingly bright green plot of imported, carefully nurtured lawn.

One building was a "mess hall." But it was a far cry from a couple of mess halls that came to my mind. Tasteful decor, white linen and large expanses of glass enhanced the atmosphere, while excellent food was catered for the most exacting appetites. It was all provided at no cost to us.

I was happy to see an Olympic-sized pool, half of it shaded by a special roof. There were a first-rate nightclub, a movie theater, bowling alleys, schools and, finally our *barrasti* (sleeping quarters for men without families)—and all of this was blessed with air conditioning.

Although I could have had quarters to myself, I preferred to share my *barrasti* and was assigned to a pleasant room with another American. Rusty was little older than I and had been in Arabia more than a year. He was the president of the company employee association.

My job took a great deal of concentration and kept me busy. The offices were filled with pleasant, able people. If you weren't competent, you didn't last here. There were only two directions to go: upward or out.

Here, too, were the fascinations of Arabia itself. Burnoosed Arabs, veiled women and desert Bedouins would appear magically out of the silent sand wherever we stopped our balloon-tired company cars along the roadless way to the distant oil fields. Gradually, Arabic phrases began to creep into our conversation.

One afternoon while two other company men and I were walking near the main gate of the nearest Arab city, we noticed a crowd gathering. We arrived at the fringe of the crowd in time to see an Arab being held down with his arm stretched out and his hand tied flat on a large wooden block. The man's face showed no emotion. The crowd grew silent and expectant. Another Arab stepped forward, threw his burnoose back from his arms and, with a swift motion, swung aloft something that gleamed metallically in the sunset. It was a huge, 2-handed scimitar.

He brought it down through flesh and bone until it bit deep into the block behind the completely severed hand. This hand, tied on the block, quivered spasmodically several times, then lay still. Its owner had emitted only one short, hoarse, controlled scream. Then he looked dumbly for a moment, longingly, from the hand to his stump, from which shot forth a bright geyser of blood. The victim slumped backward, and his friends rushed to help him, obscuring him from our view.

This was the punishment accorded a first-offense thief. A second offense called for severance of the other hand and a foot. Decapitation was the punishment for a third offense. There were no "habitual criminals"—the United States' designation of fourth-time offenders— in Arabia. The Arabs carried out their capital punishment in the open —attendance was compulsory. It was not done with rehearsed routine behind prison walls and barred gates, with admission limited to a select few and by permission only, as is the ritual in our country in states that still have the death penalty.

Probably the Arabian theory is that punishment meted out in public serves as a warning, possibly even as a deterrent. But it is about as much of a deterrent as the various gas chambers, gallows, electric chairs and firing squads in America, where the capital crime rate increases each year. Arabs stole everything they could lay their hands on, even items that were hot or nailed down. In the case of second offenders, it was everything they could lay their hand on, but they still stole.

My two friends and I, sickened by what we had seen, cost the company nothing for our food that night. Instead, we went to the Patio, the nightclub with the dance floor under the stars and swallowed several double shots, wondering if we could keep them down.

Finally, my mind was taken off the grisly memories by animated conversation concerning a projected floor show. It was to be a presentation of company talent. As in any large group, there was talent galore—solo singers and groups, a magic act, acrobats, tumbling and dancing. I volunteered to be master of ceremonies. That night rehearsals started; in two weeks the show was ready.

On opening night, the club was packed. Aramco already had a fine Italian dance orchestra, and the club was provided with the most modern sound systems and spotlights. The show was going extremely well. I was introducing an act, when a loud, feminine voice cried, "I know you . . . you're Bill Sewell."

With the spotlight in my eyes, I could barely make out a tall figure striding toward the stage. The background music had stopped; everyone was waiting to see what was coming next. Then the lights were turned up.

"Flo!" I exclaimed happily. This was a girl I used to swim with at the Los Angeles Athletic Club. Might as well make this a visit, I thought, as long as my uninhibited friend had already stopped the show. "What are you doing here?"

"Operating a comptometer and swimming too, of course. Every chance I get. Hey . . ." she interrupted herself. "You better go on with the show. You're doing pretty well for a swimmer out of water."

"See you afterward," I told her as the house applauded good-naturedly. The show went well, but I was happy when it ended and I could renew an old acquaintance. Shortly afterwards, Flo and I formed swimming teams, held meets in which interest was added by the presence of two former American Olympic team male divers, also working for Aramco, and gave the children lessons. We took on teams from other Aramco-built communities, Ras El Mishab, Ras El Tunura and Abqaic. Flo was a real competitor and asked me to coach her in regular workouts. Then she got the idea of staging a full-scale water show.

With company backing, we worked hard to make it a success. There were to be water ballet groups, with wives and daughters of employees as well as girl office workers, and a stage show. We had pictures and stories in the company newspaper, *The Aramco News*, which, like everything in the company, was well-staffed. It had professional reporters and photographers. Finally we had programs printed and sent out invitations to the other company cities.

A gigantic, glamorous water show—staged in the middle of the Arabian Desert. That's what it was, and it was pronounced a glowing success.

I literally had it made. I had been in Arabia for a year, and had spent a 4-week, expense-paid vacation in India. I had been promoted three times until I was supervising a large staff of office personnel and was earning in excess of a thousand dollars a month—which was all banked, as there was no way for me to spend it. I had formed fine friendships. Under the Aramco retirement plan, I could leave at the end of fifteen years, at an early age, with approximately half-salary for the rest of my life, in addition to the huge nest egg I couldn't help but accumulate.

Still, it wasn't for me. For the second time since San Quentin, I was set for life. But I had an itch I couldn't scratch. I wasn't dissatisfied or ungrateful. But inside me there seemed to be a drive toward something, something that would count for more than merely making a comfortable place for myself. What it was and what it meant, I didn't know.

I confided to Flo in the midst of one of our strenuous workouts. She had been swimming in the Persian Gulf, concentrating on distance and endurance instead of speed. I had been coaching her, although I couldn't see why she put herself through this daily grind when the events in our swimming meets were sprints. But I enjoyed it and didn't question her motives.

"I understand how you feel," she said when I told her I was resigning. "It took me time to figure out just where I fit in, but now I've found it.

"Bill, this is a secret still. But I'm going to swim the English Channel. I know I can do it. All I need is a couple of months more practice. I sure wish you could stay and continue to help. When I have made the Channel and have earned a real place for myself in swimming, then I want to devote my life to working with children—blind, handicapped, any kind of youngsters, in swimming."

"Gee, Flo," I said slowly, not wanting to dampen her high spirits, but at the same time thinking of that treacherous and forbidding stretch of cold, choppy water she wanted to conquer. "I hate to say it, but you know you're not a teen-ager anymore, and well, Flo, you know a lot of men have died trying that swim. Can't you do something else?"

"No, Bill, I can't," she said slowly, disappointed in my reaction. "I can't do something else any more than you can stay here and be content. I'm sure I'll make it."

"I hope we're still friends," I told her earnestly. "I just don't want to encourage you in something that may kill you. And to be absolutely honest, I really don't think you can make it. It's just too much."

"I will make it. I've made up my mind. I'm like you. I would rather die trying than not try at all."

When I left, a number of friends came down to the airport to see me off, Flo among them. She was sorry to be saying good-bye but hopeful about my future and still highly optimistic about her own.

"Don't worry," she called out. "I'm not about to drown. You'll read about it in the newspapers."

And I did. Just a few months later, Florence Chadwick successfully swam the English Channel.

Obviously I could have abandoned my search for a place in life then and there and become a sports forecaster!

8

Lima, Peru was lovely, a gem of a metropolis reposing at the foot of the western Andes near the sparkling sea. The city has lush green growth the year-round, but never a drop of rain. The abundance of growing things is due to the waters constantly descending from the towering mountains. According to its latitude and longitude and its relation to the ocean's warm water currents, Lima should be inhumanly hot and stifling from October to June. Yet it is always light-suit weather. This condition is evidently due to a curious phenomenon, a large circular cloud that hangs above the city throughout the summer months and disappears only with the coming of cooler weather.

Everything about Lima fascinated me (which was fortunate, since I landed without sufficient money to get back to the United States).

Since leaving Arabia two years before, I had been around the world several times, allowing circumstances and whatever funds I had saved in Arabia to dictate my itinerary. My return to India led to interviews with Nehru; as a matter of fact, I was set to manage a construction project in India—when the policy switched to "India for Indians," and many foreigners who had been there for years and considered India their home, lost their jobs. I never got mine. There was a brief fling in the export-import business, and the intrigue involved when I undertook to transport a valuable packet of gems from Delhi to Rome. There were Paris and Brussels and Madrid, and travels through my own country which led me from New York to Oregon, from Montana to Mississippi, from Florida to Alaska. I had sold real estate and house trailers, pots and pans, books and ideas. I had worked as a concrete vibrator operator on Hungry Horse Dam near Whitefish, Montana, as a construction boss and signalman for a cableway. But it—that elusive "it"—was not to be found in any of these projects.

Now I was in South America.

I had struck up an acquaintance on the plane with Juan Paez, a bullfighter destined to become famous. He was doing his best to teach me Spanish. One day he found an ad in the Spanish newspaper and explained there was a good job open for a Spanish-speaking American. I had only half the qualifications, so I asked him to translate the remainder of the ad. Pan American-Grace Airways needed a man to manage five jungle airports and a hotel in Bolivia, along the route the airline took from Lima to the east coast cities of Rio de Janeiro, Montevideo and Buenos Aires.

I asked Juanito the Spanish words for "What do you want me to say?" Then I put on my most conservative suit and tie and set out for the airline offices.

Once there, everything went smoothly and it looked as if I had the job. However, at the last moment, the Spanish-speaking American interviewing me suddenly asked, "*¿Habla español, señor?*"

"*Sí, yo hablo español,*" I replied with what I hoped was a confident smile.

"*Dígame,*" he went on.

"*¿Qué quiere usted que yo diga?*" This was the one phrase I had learned from Juanito.

"Your references from Aramco and San Bernardino County are excellent, so I feel that you will suit us admirably, Mr. Sewell," he said, fortunately in English. I was hired.

I was flying under false colors that day in respect to my knowledge of Spanish. But a month later I was not, because in the hinterlands I went to, the only languages spoken besides Spanish were Indian dialects. During the interim I had become known as "*El Jefe Un Momento.*" This was because I carried a little Spanish-English dictionary in my breast pocket. Every time I came to an impasse (about a hundred times a day) I would hold up a hand and adjure "*un momento*" until I had consulted the little volume and could continue the conversation.

This took place in Santa Cruz, a jungle outpost community on the exact, geometric center of the South American continent. We were flown there from Lima, up until we were high enough to make it through a pass in the Andes, a pass where the deep snows are permanent, lying in the shadows of the upthrust escarpments. Lake Titicaca, the highest large body of water in the world, sparkled below us like acres of diamonds.

The passengers in the old C-47 had been supplied oxygen masks, and when we landed for an overnight stop at Bolivia's capital, La Paz, I wished I had brought my mask with me from the plane. When the door was opened the stewardess did not say, "Take a deep breath." But it would have been helpful. At the 14,000-foot-high landing field, there seemed to be no oxygen to breathe. In the 100-foot walk from the plane to the passenger terminal, there was not one of us who didn't stop, gasping and straining, to suck in enough air to make it to the building.

Santa Cruz, at a much lower altitude was a sizable old community of about 25,000 persons, surrounded for a radius of ten miles by lush green farms and ranches, literally hacked from the jungle. The airport, at the edge of farm country, abutted hard against the thick tropical forest. As seen from the air, my new home was quite impressive. The low, modern buildings surrounding the huge courtyard made up the hotel complex, and I could see the 3-story penthouse tower in which I would have a furnished apartment.

The sight was even more impressive when the plane door was opened and we stepped out into the balmy Santa Cruz air. Waiting at the airport apron were two long lines of anxious-looking Spanish men and women. They turned out to be the staff I had inherited, some 120 in all. They had been rehearsed about my pending arrival. Now they stood, dressed in their Sunday-best, apprehensive, looking in my direction.

At the bottom of the gangway, four men introduced themselves. One was the Grace Shipping Company representative. The two dispatchers, Ken and Tom, were Americans. The local station manager, a Spaniard called "Mac," made a flowery Spanish speech of welcome.

These preliminaries over, I was escorted down the line of waiting employees. My predecessor, I understood, had been something of a martinet, and heaven knows what they expected of their new *jefe*. I wanted to put them at ease, so I shook hands cordially with each one.

Mac took care of my baggage and showed me to my quarters. There was a spacious living room with polished mahogany furniture. On the floor was an enormous jaguar-skin rug with mounted head. The bedroom was almost as large. French doors provided access to wide balconies off each room—one with a view of the airfield, the other overlooking the attractive patio.

As I returned to the lobby to check on my luggage the serenity of the hotel was shattered for the day. A sudden shriek, loud enough to awaken every mummy in Egypt, pierced the air. It was a scream of mortal terror. The lobby turned into a tableau of frozen figures. I ran for the stairway, followed by Ken, Tom and half the staff. At the entrance to my apartment we found an American woman tourist, who had just passed my open door.

"It moved, it moved, it moved!" she screamed. She was pointing to the jaguar-skin rug.

"It—what?" The fact that my eardrums and nervous system had both been destroyed in the same instant didn't help.

Tom and Ken were more sympathetic. They patted the woman and led her to a chair. Then they started looking in corners, behind furniture. When they went into the other room and looked under the bed, they let out a couple of words that weren't in my Spanish dictionary. Tom dragged out an obviously terrified, full-grown, spitting ocelot. Shaking his finger and repeating over and over "*Malo, malo, malo!*" Tom hauled the 100-pound creature by the scruff of its neck out of the room.

The ocelot was their pet and completely docile, they explained, virtually on their knees before the woman. He had the run of the place and apparently identified with several jaguar-skin rugs, for he used to nap on them by the hour. He must have been there, his spots blending with those of his distant, dead relative, when my earlier entrance had disturbed him.

The following day I began my official duties. These included computing the load balance and distribution of passengers, fuel and baggage on all of our flights (which I did with a kind of slide rule), greeting any VIPs and flying out once a week to our four other airports, each about an hour distant by air. My assignment also made me chief liaison officer for the company and its official representative to the Bolivian Government.

My predecessor had things well organized. Although my title of "senior operations representative" made me the sole administrative head of all the five Panagra airports in Bolivia, with full responsibility for their maintenance and operation, everything had been departmentalized and organized so that a competent person headed each department. The top chef, for instance, not only supervised the kitchen but also ordered the food, supplies and equipment. The head maid supervised the staff of girls, the chief waitress did an admirable job in the dining room, the mechanics knew their business, Tom and Ken handled the radio and dispatching chores and Mac acted as my administrative assistant and did most of the actual managing of the Santa Cruz Station.

My job was one of public relations for the staff with the towns-people. I tried to run the place as fairly as possible and, as my policy became known, the staff started coming to me with all kinds of personal problems.

There was just enough administrative work to keep life from being indolent. I had free time to travel around the countryside. I watched the fascinating and never-ending fight of the ranchers and farmers to hold back the encroaching jungle. With Tom and Ken I hunted python, jaguar and wild boar. I became friends with the local banker (who gave me a spirited horse to ride on my trips into the jungle), was entertained by the rich ranchers and dined as graciously in the homes of some of my employees.

Life was beautiful. San Quentin might never have been. For the third time in a brief span of years, I had it made. Good friends, loyal employees, a fine job which allowed me to bank my entire monthly salary. I was set for life.

What more could any man want?

But it palled. I wasn't sufficiently articulate to clarify my thoughts, or perhaps they were not yet ready for crystallization. All I knew was that I didn't want to sit in some corner of the world, accepting luxuries as my due and accomplishing nothing more than a comfortable existence. What would I have to show for it at the end of my life? A string of crazy adventures and a stack of material possessions?

I resigned my position with Panagra, and after an emotional farewell with my staff, returned to Lima.

There I heard that the United States Embassy was looking for someone to organize and direct a program of water sports for Peruvian youth. I went to the Embassy, talked to the attaché on cultural affairs, gave him my credentials and awaited developments. The Embassy recommended me for the job, on a lend-lease basis under which the United States Government would pay half of my salary. I was then interviewed by Peruvian Government officials and accepted.

Then it struck me. This was the same job I had held in Bombay, in a way, and I wasn't satisfied with that for a lifework. What made me think I would be happier now? Obviously, I wouldn't be. So I secured a satisfactory replacement, a man better qualified than I to run the sports program. Then I resigned, bought a ticket and left for the States.

> WANTED: Young men and women, good co-ordination, as dance teachers. No exp. nec. We will train.

Thus I became a dance teacher at Arthur Murray's in Fresno, California. (I had been staying there with friends until I could figure out my next move.) Arthur Murray's gave me an education that was to last the rest of my life. Here, in addition to learning just about every dance step ever invented, I really learned how to sell.

I had always considered myself a pretty accomplished salesman. But only at Murray's did I learn the meaning of the word. I learned about negative selling, emotional selling, promotion, public relations and the art of selling the intangible, the idea, the dream. This was the way it had to be. Nobody beats your door down to pay out more than $7,000 for a lifetime course of dance lessons. And I sold six of these in six weeks.

My reward was a trip to Acapulco. But I valued the real prize I had won far more. I reread all the books on positive thought that I had studied at San Quentin. It was like going through allegories on life, such as *Alice in Wonderland* and *Gulliver's Travels*, as an adult, after having read them originally as a child.

That was what I prized most: the impetus I was given to reapply myself to the art of positive thinking and the lessons I learned about selling.

Eventually, I opened my own dance studio. I lacked money, but I had plenty of ideas and good friends willing to help. My teaching system differed widely from Arthur Murray's but was not at cross-purposes to it. The town was certainly big enough to hold us both. I leased a building that had hardwood floors, and swapped future dance lessons for other installations. Now that I had my own business, I wanted to set down certain rules as my own. I emphasized these at our staff meetings:

"There are only two directions a teacher can go—up or out (Aramco). I won't tolerate any office politics or tattling to me or anyone else about anything that goes on here (San Quentin). The only way to advance is to push the person ahead of you higher up the ladder and pull up the person behind you. That way you have a friend on top pulling and a friend below pushing. An attempt to get promoted by any other means will be met with a firing—and everyone will be present to witness it (my own). If you have any problems you think I can help you with, I'll be glad to try and, of course, everything will be in the strictest confidence (Panagra)."

I was captain of my own little ship again and it was a happy ship.

To accommodate the rush of students I was expanding as rapidly as possible. But it took a great deal of money—and a great many hours of my time—just to keep pace with the flourishing business. It was becoming an inverted pyramid—with more teachers, more office help, more equipment, more students, more of everything, except of me. Twenty-one hours a day on the job, seven days a week, were barely enough for me to get everything done.

As in any other explosive expansion, unforeseen difficulties proved costly. Then, there was personnel. Like Chrissy.

Chrissy was a naïve little Spanish girl, not more than 17 years old when I first met her while she was teaching at Arthur Murray's. After I opened the new studio she not only taught dancing but took a side job as a waitress so she could contribute her tip money to help me get started. Solid.

The graceful and gracious little Chrissy had the longest waiting line of any instructor in the studio. Even after I established the policy that any student who wanted lessons from this premium teacher had to take a minimum of two hundred hours—a cash outlay of $2,000 —the waiting line kept right on growing.

She didn't regard the dance studio as work. It was her home away from home, since her mother lived in Albuquerque. Then one night she brought me her "young man." I approved, and six weeks later she was married. And I lost my best teacher.

There was the girl I'll call Diane. Like Chrissy, she was with the studio from the beginning. Diane was beautiful, with a sparkling warmth and spirit that shone in her eyes, glowed in her conversation and her bright smile. She was popular, an excellent teacher, a wonderful exhibition ballroom dancer, and she had a high degree of intelligence and initiative. She was a natural for the job of manager of a branch studio in her hometown, some fifty miles distant. Ecstatic when I gave her the news, she rushed home to tell her family and friends.

But she never made it.

"Did you hear about Diane?" It was one of my teachers on the telephone early the next morning. She was sobbing. "She was in an accident. In her car. It's terrible. . . ."

"Is she hurt badly?"

"They don't think she'll live. She's all cut to pieces. Dear God, and she was so beautiful. . . ."

I tore over to the hospital. Diane was in a deep coma. Information from the doctor was disheartening. In addition to a score of serious injuries, she had fractures of the skull and severe brain damage. He doubted that she would recover.

At the studio, dance lessons had to go on as usual. But the foxtrot and rhumba rhythms might as well have been the notes of the dirge as far as the teachers were concerned. Daily we sent messages, cards and flowers. But Diane didn't know of them. It was weeks before the doctor finally could tell us she was going to live. What should have been wonderful news, however, was taken very quietly by all of us. For in answer to our previous inquiries about injuries to her face, the doctor had said simply:

"It's gone."

I visited her the first day she was home. Her parents, who had been in prayerful seclusion, were reluctant to let me in. But I finally persuaded them to let me see her. There was pain.

But not for Diane. She felt nothing, saw nothing, heard nothing —knew nothing. I didn't realize this, though, as I controlled my own expression. No nose, one side of her face dragged down and distorted, the other side punched in where bone as well as flesh was gone, her mouth twisted out of shape.

I didn't think I had a tear in my entire makeup, but I felt them falling like big drops of rain on the coverlet when I took her hands and called her name. There was no response. I was knocking on a door where no one was at home.

But Diane's doctor had assured me that there was hope. As far as I was concerned "Where there's hope, there's life." Each day one of my dance teachers would accompany me to the house; there we would talk to Diane and play dance music on the record player. Her father or I would carry her to the living room and sit her in a big chair, then a teacher and I would give a showy exhibition of the dances Diane had loved.

There is a special place in my heart for the throbbing rhythm of "La Comparsita," because it was to this stirring tango that Diane first showed any reaction. That was the day something moved at the hem of her long housecoat. Diane was trying to tap her foot.

From that time on we turned that record player up to its limit of volume. The entire county must have rocked to the strains of "La Comparsita." For some reason this particular piece of music fanned a tiny spark to life in Diane's brain. Soon her foot could keep time to the music. When I sat down to have a cigarette between dances, Diane made a little vocal noise and pursed her lips. Her glazed eyes were trying to focus in the general direction of the glowing end of my cigarette. I placed it between her scarred lips, and found it was what she wanted. She couldn't puff on it, but it had struck a chord somewhere deep inside her. It was familiar. Such simple things, tango music and a cigarette. How much they meant to the almost annihilated spirit that was struggling so desperately to live again.

I'll never forget the day Diane managed her first real puff on a cigarette. She inhaled and coughed. But something wonderful happened—Diane laughed.

Then Diane's religious relatives began to nag that she was reaping the wages of sin—of dancing and smoking, even of having cocktails. That day I swept her up in my arms and carried her to my sports car, strapped her in with a safety belt and took her for a long fast ride. The wind streamed against her face and ruffled her dark hair, cropped and newly grown after the brain operations.

Every day after that I would pick her up and, carrying her so that her toes barely touched the floor, would dance with her. Though wasted and frail, she actually began to try to keep step. Every day we went for a ride in the open car. When I found she would give a little laugh when we went around fast corners, I would curve like a madman.

The time came when we—my teachers and I—had done as much as any layman could. Diane could understand. She was beginning to make herself understood. Some of her first efforts were clumsy, but she would laugh at her mistakes. Even her frightful sensitivity when she saw herself in the mirror served a purpose. The time had come for plastic surgeons and other specialists to take over Diane.

It was a long process, restoring that face to anything like its former beauty. Years of operations. The expenses were fantastic. But they were all met. The entire town of Madera turned out to help courageous Diane. Service clubs had collection cans in every bank and restaurant and public place. And some of the money came from the Sewell Dance Studios Benefit Party given in conjunction with the local 20-30 Club.

Due to a whole set of new circumstances, I could not watch her progress. Years later, I decided to see her. Last summer I drove to the Pacific Coast, found out where she lived and presented myself at the front door of her lovely suburban home. The last time I had seen Diane she had no memory of the accident that crippled her—two teen-agers racing on the wrong side of a divided highway had forced her car off the road and against a tree. Now, as I rang her doorbell, I wondered if she would remember me.

There she was in the doorway. Beautiful—again.

"Bill!" With a happy cry she launched herself at me. "You made me smoke a cigarette and tap my foot." What a freakish thing the human memory can be! How could she have pulled those little things from the leaden cloud that obscured her world during those days? "And you carried me around the floor to try to make me dance!"

"How do you know all that?" I asked when I could get my breath.

"How do I know?" She laughed in delight. "Because I was there, silly. That was the first time anyone ever had to carry me on a dance floor—and there wasn't anything I could do about it. I remember you came and you talked to me and you cried." Her voice went soft as she saw I was crying again. But there was a world of difference now.

Diane showed me her home and her three children, then told me about her husband. "He's a doll," she said happily.

An acquaintance I had looked up in my search for her had told me glowing things about her.

"That girl, Diane, went to live with her sister, closer to town. After the last operation, the doctors told her it was up to her from then on. Well, Diane set herself a goal. She made up her mind to walk to town and back every day. That's thirteen blocks down and thirteen blocks back. And she did it. At first, she used to stumble and fall. But she'd always pick herself up—sometimes real slow and painful-like and go on. Her clothes would be dusty and her knees skinned where she'd fallen down, and her balance would be off sometimes —so she'd kinda weave like. But she'd be walking. And she'd always be ahummin' some tune—Mexican music, it sounded like. . . ."

She was humming it now as she ran to put on coffee. I followed her to the kitchen and picked up the strains of the music she hummed. All at once the kitchen was a ballroom, and we were tangoing again to "La Comparsita."

Then I left, but I will see her again.

Incidentally, among those I met in the dance studio were three former high school buddies. One, Billy Vukovich, took some dancing lessons and in return taught me some of the finer points of race car driving. I became a sports car addict. He invited me to become a member of his crew at Indianapolis the following year, but I'm glad I bowed out. On the way to his third win in succession that year, he crashed and perished—the way he had said he wanted to go when his time came.

Ross Bagdasarian was another former schoolmate. He had written "C'mon a' My House" and "Hey, Brother, Pour the Wine." He was forming his own record company and making a recording that no one else had any faith in, "The Chipmunk Song." He used the name David Seville on that one.

But it was a third classmate who had the most profound effect on me. I'll call him Dr. George. It was to him that I went when

I began to feel as if I were coming apart. The twenty-one-hour days and seven-day weeks had begun to tell. The only relaxation I had had in almost a year were my visits to Diane. Dr. George put me through all the tests and then sat me down for a talk.

"How much does this dance business mean to you?" he asked.

I explained it was my livelihood and one I enjoyed.

"Does it mean more to you than your life?" He added soberly, "Keep at it for another ninety days and that will be your life. All of it. You are suffering from mental, nervous and physical exhaustion. You don't have more than ninety days to live, unless you get out and rest up—for a long time."

I did as he advised. Resigned, sold out. After a heartbreaking farewell to my staff, I bought a lovely, white-hulled forty-six-foot yacht and lolled on it for six months. I wore sandals and striped T-shirts but refrained from growing a beard. Finally, I went back to Dr. George, who seemed well pleased that I was about to die of boredom instead of exhaustion. He gave me the green light to resume living.

The most obvious thing to do first, of course, was to go on a diamond-hunting expedition into the unexplored jungles of Venezuela.

9

THE EXPEDITION THAT FOLLOWED MY NEAR breakdown was destined to be a marked contrast to the sedentary life I'd been leading on my yacht. I had been fascinated by an article in *Argosy* magazine. about diamonds in South America. Diamonds in Africa are formed in flues as a result of volcanic pressures. In African mines, diamonds are usually discovered in the flues and mined from shafts.

In Venezuela, according to the article, the volcanic flues were formed by the upthrusting Andes Mountains. But the diamonds were washed away by torrential tropical rains. The incredible deluges of that clime through the ages had spread the diamonds like a carpet for hundreds of miles through the lowland jungles. Sometimes, digging in their backyards, natives have found whole pockets. Yet in the same region, one could dig for ten miles and never uncover one. With optimism based on my usual serendipitous experiences, I figured on finding at least one pocket.

To my surprise and delight, my friend Scott offered to go with me. Scott was a doctor of entomology with a master's degree in geology. He was an ex-paratrooper—six-foot-five of whalebone and muscle.

Without ever having been there, there was little Scott did not know of our destination. We were heading for the Lost World country of Devil's Mountain, in the unpenetrated wilds of the interior of Venezuela. According to all the information we could get, no man, native or otherwise, had set foot in that forbidding tangle of growth.

Accordingly, we made elaborate preparations. Scott made up two complete first-aid kits. They contained (in addition to standard gauze, tape and dressings) antibiotics that could be applied to wounds, taken orally or injected by hypodermic needle, plus syringes, drugs for pain, a complete snake kit (including antivenin) and finally, scalpels, hemostats, sutures and needles. Coincidentally, both of us had assisted in surgery somewhere along the line, Scott in college and I in the hospital at Preston.

We also packed short-handled shovels, small pickaxes, flashlights, canteens, jungle hammocks and machetes.

There was no use including firearms of any kind. Venezuela was in a state of political unrest, with threats of revolution in the air; therefore, possession of firearms by any but police and army was forbidden. We flew from San Francisco to Miami to Caracas, the oil-affluent capital city of Venezuela. Then we went by Avensa Airways from Caracas to Ciudad Bolivar, a beautiful city on the Orinoco River and the last outpost of civilization. Here we took a small chartered plane across what seemed like endless miles of jungle to a savannah the pilot called Chiguao. This was indeed the end of the line. We let it be known in the savannah's native village that we would pay well for a guide to take us at least part of the way. The natives were friendly, cordial and pleasant—and they all said No.

They obliged us in every other way, however, with information about the country. But when it came to accompanying us, each had a tale of an aunt or an uncle or a brother who had been eaten by *El Tigre*—the jaguar. Apparently the tales were not exaggerated. We found verification among the several outsiders who lived in the savannah: a German engineer, a Dutch diamond buyer and several Spaniards, who, like ourselves, were in search of diamonds. These men informed us that the jaguar was truly lord of this jungle. Now, with all firearms confiscated, none of the natives were willing to risk running into *El Tigre*.

At last, by promising we would leave all of our expensive gear with him as a bonus, we induced one stalwart Indian to come with us. This settled, we inquired how we would recognize a diamond when we saw it.

"Ah, señor, not to worry. You will know, señor, you will know," was the universal answer.

The next morning, after camping in the open savannah without incident, we started off with our stalwart guide, whom we called "Shorty." Entering the jungle was like stepping from day into twilight, even though the tropical sun was beating down brightly in the clearing. Vines and bushes grew everywhere between the towering trees, and great elephantine leaves and giant ferns impeded our progress. And everywhere there was life, flying and crawling and slithering and screaming, living and dying all around us.

The 140-pound packs Scott and I carried forced us to stop frequently. Once, when I was leaning against a conveniently low branch, Scott uttered a warning cry. I straightened just in time—the branch was alive with huge hairy spiders. The next time, a branch by Scott's head seemed too brilliant a green, even for this multihued forest. As I pointed to it, we saw a snake of the mamba family take himself off in a series of rapid esses.

It was late in the day when we reached the spot we had decided upon from the airplane. It was beside a jungle stream, near a declivity in the ground that seemed to be a likely place for diamonds to collect. The jungle grew right to the water's edge, and here we camped, stringing our hammocks across our homemade clearing.

The next morning we began our search for diamonds. The method was to put shovelsful of dirt in our *surukus* (three-layered sieves we had obtained in the village), then to pour water over them while we ran our hands through the trapped earth and rocks. The circular screens, set one above the other, were of different weaves—the finest was at the bottom. Chunks that passed through the first coarse screening were thus caught by the next one and so on.

It was tedious work. We dug several holes, some to a depth of six feet, during our first day. Because the diamonds had been scattered and washed over for thousands of years, it was almost like throwing a dart at a map.

The next three nights and days were repetitions of the first. On our fourth evening, we had some diversion. We had finished supper, and twilight had turned into jungle night. Suddenly the native grabbed us and began to chatter in a complete panic. Finally he got out something we could understand: "*El Tigre! El Tigre!*"

We whirled to face the jungle, trying to penetrate the green wall with our flashlights. But we saw nothing and we heard only the usual noises of the night. I asked Shorty in Spanish, "How do you know—what tells you?" He pointed to his nose. "*Olfacto. Olfacto. Sí, El Tigre.*"

Then, even our civilization-blunted sense of smell caught it. The rank odor of cat, big cat. The stench was full upon us. We made a hasty plan. There was no time to build a big fire. We would sit on the ground in the center of our open spot, back to back, with our knees pulled up and braced against each other. In front of us, we would hold our machetes. It was our hope that one of the machetes could be thrust into *El Tigre's* underbelly, if he leaped high enough in his attack. The man who took to the trees to outclimb a jaguar would do just as well to take to the open fields to try to outrun a greyhound. It wasn't much of a bastion, but the best we could manage with the means on hand. We hunched together, our flashlights turned off. On my count of three, Scott and I were to turn on our powerful lamps and each would sweep his half of the circle. Shorty was useless, paralyzed with fear.

"One," I could feel the tense muscles in the back braced against my own, "two, three."

There was *El Tigre*, all six feet of him, ahead in my light beam—not twenty feet away.

As the light glared, he snarled hideously. His saber teeth gleamed and his eyes blazed like two giant topaz gems. His tail switched down toward its tip. My belly would be tender and soft to those 3-inch teeth and talons. I tried to hug my legs a little closer against me and tightened my grip on the machete.

"I got him—dead ahead of me," I murmured.

"Yeah, I figured," Scott's low voice answered.

Then—like that—he was gone. Gone without a sound through undergrowth so dense a rabbit would have snapped twigs and vines getting through.

The instant the big cat disappeared, Shorty jumped to his feet, completely calm and satisfied, even exuberant. Scott and I, however, were prepared to hold our positions for the remainder of the night. The native insisted the danger was over. When the jaguar left without attacking, it meant he wasn't hungry. When I finally decided to stand up, my muscles were so tense that cramps had set in, and I was sore for days thereafter. Scott was in the same condition, and we hobbled around like a couple of arthritic oldsters.

We spent two more nights in the jungle and another two weeks poking around in the ground of the savannah. And one day we found what we sought. There it lay in the sand, flashing like—a diamond! For some reason, I had always thought diamonds in the raw were black. It had been my understanding that the brilliance was the result of cutting and polishing. Of course, this one didn't look like a gem in Cartier's, but the unmistakable hard luster was there. And, it was diamond-shaped.

We unearthed five more diamonds before we ran out of money. I realize that statement, containing those two pieces of information, doubtless should go down in history as a warning, not an example. Nevertheless, it was a fact. Our six small diamonds, worth approximately $400 in the United States, according to the diamond buyer on the scene, represented a great deal more than the average find for the time we had spent there. It meant a lot more to Scott and me to take them home in their raw state than it did for us to sell them to the local buyer and go on with the search. Besides, the thrill was in the finding, not in the value of the find (unless, of course, a fabulous fortune were to have been unearthed). But there had been none made in these fields, we heard, so we picked up our diamonds and went home.

Since the $400 was our return on an investment of several thousand dollars, it behooved me to find something profitable to do—and fast.

Back in the United States, I took the first job that seemed suitable, that of a public relations man for Continental Airlines. New duties took me to Denver, then to Tulsa. In Tulsa, I met a phenomenal individual, whom I will call Chuck.

Still under thirty, Chuck already had amassed a multimillion-dollar fortune, starting only three years before with a borrowed $800. He was a mathematical genius. He had started as a construction engineer. Somewhere along the line, he had found he could estimate correctly, in about one-twelfth the time it would take the usual estimator, all costs, materials and time a project would require. When I met him, he was sole owner of several large companies. He had contracts for most of the schools, hospitals and highways being built in the state. Now he wanted to build a dance studio, not just the building, but the entire works. He was a dance addict, and I saw an opportunity to help some of my former teachers.

After I had staffed his new studio and launched it successfully, Chuck told me he had a yen to build dams and that he understood great plans were going forward along these lines in South America. When I told him my history there, he made me vice-president of two of his companies. My specific assignment was to be in charge of sales and contracts.

As we left for Latin America, he made a mistake that was to cost him dearly. He had fallen in love with one of the dance teachers I had sent for from the West Coast. Never had I seen two people more suited for one another. They were married in Los Angeles, and then we were off.

Back to Caracas, Ciudad Bolivar and Lima. My past connections there proved invaluable, chiefly because I was able to follow the prescribed Latin formula for transacting business. We were awarded a total of $33 million in contracts for a dam, a hospital, a cement plant and roads.

We raced back to the United States to fulfill the contracts, only to discover Chuck had no companies. His wife had taken over their ownership through legal action, then disposed of their assets. That's right, his wife. Not the former dance teacher who accompanied us to

South America, but the wife he had not divorced before he married the dancer. Oh boy, for the life of a genius, I thought, as I started job-hunting again.

Next I went to work as a sales consultant, to rejuvenate the sales staff of a home reducing machine manufacturer. My work for the reducing people led me eventually to the national headquarters of Silhouette Home Plan International, Inc., in Beverly Hills. Through the grapevine—San Quentin has no copyright on it—I learned that this outfit was in financial trouble.

When I walked in the door of their Beverly Hills headquarters, I understood what was happening to their money. The display was ostentatious, from the thick pile underfoot, the Picasso originals, the Italian silks covering the walls to the gigantic neon map of the United States that hung from the ceiling in the directors' room. Full of winking lights, the map boasted four clocks for the various time zones. In front of this spectacle were four uniformed girls wearing telephone headsets for the projected purpose of receiving customers' calls from all over the nation. The entire premise was fantastic, since their only branch offices were on the West Coast—and they weren't doing any business.

My interview with the two bosses of this spending safari convinced me it was necessary to play chess with these characters. They were losing approximately $50,000 a month, according to the grapevine. What they needed was a man who could pull them out of the red and make the business of selling home reducing machines profitable. After studying their sales, personnel, payroll, the machine itself, I told them that if I were given a free hand, it might be possible to pull them out in six months. Meanwhile I could reduce the outgo by at least 60 percent.

They offered me $2,000 a month salary and $5 a unit override on every machine sold, plus certain travel expenses. But I needed some method to make them keep their word. The salary offered no particular problem, but when sales started to mount I knew this pair would want to pocket all the profits by persuading me to accept only the salary. What I needed, of course, was a written contract. But I had a better chance of selling a reducing machine on Mars than of getting those two committed on paper. I had heard that doing business with them was like getting a grip on quicksilver.

Nevertheless, two days later I presented myself in their offices, and accepted the job. We shook hands and had a drink on it. Just before leaving, I said in my most guileless tone:

"This damned travel expense is so ramified. I'd like to make an outline of it on paper. Otherwise I'll be figuring on money coming to me that isn't properly due or . . . what the hell, let's put something down on paper we can all refer to. . . ."

The narrowed eyes widened again when I asked them to summon their secretary. "I'll just dictate it off the top of my head," I said. I began, hesitantly, to dictate. Every once in a while I would pause and wait for them to supply information that momentarily escaped me. It was a short, simple agreement almost totally devoid of legal language. It took the girl only minutes to hand us all typed copies.

Then I did some of the hardest work of my life. My first edict was to close all the branch offices, thereby cutting out unearned salaries of branch managers and the enormous outgo for "front." My next move was to set up a franchise plan under which I sold exclusive sales rights in specific territories. Thus in order to make money for himself, the franchise holder had to make money for the company.

I wrote sales manuals, training manuals, taught training directors to teach the franchise holders to operate successfully, picked regional managers to supervise the training directors and put every one of them on a commission basis. No production, no pay. The result was inevitable; in less than the six months I had predicted, the company was out of the red and beginning to show a profit. Now more than one thousand people were working under my supervision, and none of them made any money unless they made the company money.

It was at about this time that I walked into the Beverly Hills headquarters to get the override monies due me—several thousand dollars.

"Now, Bill, you've been drawing your salary regularly and that's not a salary to be sneezed at. Let's not be in a hurry about your override money," said the chairman of the board.

"I've earned it and I want it—now," I told him. "Don't forget about our agreement."

The man behind the huge desk laughed. "Our attorneys could

break that agreement in five minutes. Hell, you're smart enough to have known that when you were stumbling around here trying to dictate it."

"Smarter than you think. There is a firm of attorneys in this town called Herlihy and Herlihy, of whom you may have heard. I'll guarantee your lawyer has, because they are one of the top firms of corporation attorneys in the country. They are my friends. They wrote the agreement you signed. All I did was memorize it, prior to my stumbling dictation here. They will not write an agreement they are not willing to defend in court. So I'd suggest you have your attorney call them before doing anything rash."

They paid off.

With such a beginning, it was foreseeable I wouldn't be content to stay. Not that my employers were chagrined. In fact, the opposite was true. They considered it a big joke on themselves for having underestimated me. Still, obtaining an income by having to outwit your boss is not the way to go through life.

No, big business just wasn't it. Not for me. I had worked for some of the best and worst, but even though I was interested, I felt that life—at least my life—should stand for something more than merely making money.

It seemed to me that I had had all of the things, at one time or another, that money could buy. Houses, a yacht, airplanes, fine cars, travel, the works. And many of the things money cannot buy— San Quentin, love, faith, friendship.

It also seemed to me that I had done just about everything—so why not do something else?

10

IT LOOKED AS IF I FOUND THE ANSWER TO my quest in show business.

The idea of going into show business with my own act came naturally to me in 1951. I was momentarily broke and in Los Angeles. As a favor to friends, I had just completed a stint as master of ceremonies at a function. Whenever a master of ceremonies was needed, it seemed I always volunteered for the job or was drafted for it. Moreover, I always seemed to enjoy it.

My entry into the entertainment world was as "Bill Sewell Presents Comedy with Character." Loaded down with an assortment of props that ranged from a glittering guitar and a fluorescent serape and sombrero to a fluorescent zoot-suit jacket, I sang such modern numbers as "Give My Regards to Broadway" (with straw hat and cane), "Is It True What They Say About Dixie?" (with fluorescent bow tie and gloves), "Lullaby of Broadway" (with top hat and cane) and finally, "Darktown Strutters' Ball" (with zoot suit.) I was pretty bad.

But I actually got work in various clubs in Los Angeles, and then a number of one-night stands, playing burlesque joints and smaller clubs in Carlsbad, New Mexico; Baton Rouge, Louisiana; Panama City, Florida; Marysville, California. The audiences' applause (evidently they were awed by my array of props if not my talent) gave me a warm feeling, almost a feeling of belonging. This was what I had been vainly searching for from my mother during my youth—approval, recognition. In order to please audiences, I strove valiantly to perfect my act. Gradually, I discarded my props. Luckily I found a sympathetic agent. He christened me Bill Sands, a name, he said, that was more euphonious than my own and a better length for billing. I had new photographs taken, a new brochure printed—and worked out a new act. It was my hope that no one in the entertainment field would remember Bill Sewell. I was Bill Sands, and my act was now called, in the trade, "a good, competent, professional nightclub routine." I began to play many of the leading clubs in the country.

One night, Jerry Ross, an agent in Seattle, stopped by to ask me to do one show for him at the Olympic Hotel between my performances at the Magic Inn. He took out of his briefcase an old picture of a youth in a black dinner jacket with a violent-colored serape over his shoulder, a sombrero on his head and a guitar in his hands.

"Was that you?" he asked.

"It was," I confessed with a sheepish smile.

Jerry looked at the notes he had made on the back of that picture. Then he said wryly, "I understand why you changed your name."

In the inner core of show business, I found a wonderful world with which the general public is unfamiliar. This world is inhabited by those who are in the middle class of entertainers, their fees ranging from $500 to $900 a week. They work as supporting acts for the big stars in major clubs or often as headliners in smaller but equally respectable nightclubs.

This is the world in which loyalty to one's craft is paramount. Entertainers are never late for rehearsals or performances. "The show must go on" is a way of life. And it's from this world that the real stars develop. Not the flash-in-the-pan sensations, but those who have learned their craft painstakingly, over the years, in small clubs and one-night stands. In this world, it is considered not only a breach of etiquette, but a breach of professionalism to criticize a fellow performer to any outsider. Here performance alone counts. There are no excuses and no exceptions. A "solid" world and one I understood.

While I was a resident of this world—a citizen in good standing —I met a little girl with a big voice. We teamed up together for a matter of weeks. I did the comedy, she the songs. Between shows she always asked me to let her take a few comedy lines, but I knew better than to turn a pretty girl singer into a comedienne. When later I accepted a nightclub booking for my own act across the country, my last words of advice to her were: "You have a great voice. With the right breaks you can make it as a singer. But whatever you do, forget the comedy. You just don't have what it takes to be funny."

Her name was Mimi Hines—of the now-famous team of Ford and Hines—and she is one of the funniest women in the world. So much for my advice to young people in show business.

Billy Daniels, Milton Berle, Bob Hope and other stars with whom I worked all share the same attitude toward the profession. They greet every entertainer, whether or not he has a "name," as an equal. They expect their fellow entertainers to do a professional job.

Milton Berle, for example, is known for his biting wit and sarcastic barbs that can be directed with venomous sting at a ringside heckler. When he was appearing in a New York nightclub, three women who had had too much to drink began to disrupt his routine. Berle simply walked over to the table, had a spotlight directed on the threesome, turned to the audience and asked: "Why do these

girls remind you of a baseball game? The answer," said Uncle
Miltie, "is that all three bags are loaded."

Yet, he is equally well known among entertainers as one of
the kindest men in show business. He can always be depended upon
to help someone up the ladder. His introductions of unknowns are
among the classics in the business. If I were being introduced for the
first time to a national television audience, I would rather have
Milton Berle perform the introduction than any other man in
show business.

The easy camaraderie that exists between professional entertainers—no matter what their position in show business—is illustrated
in what Bob Hope said to me when his show was broadcast from a
Lions' convention in Ontario, California.

My job was to "warm up" the audience and then to introduce
the star. Backstage, before the show, I asked him: "Mr. Hope, is
there any particular way in which you would like to be introduced?"

"You'll do a good job," he answered, "say anything you like. The
name is Hope. H-O-P-E. Hope. Now go out and knock 'em dead."

Sally Rand. Years after she had been a $10,000-a-week performer
at the Chicago World's Fair, I appeared with her in a huge barn-
like nightclub in Fort Worth, Texas. By this time my own act was
going pretty well and I was drawing good reviews. I was to open
and she was to close; in addition, I was to emcee the show. On the
opening night I took my best shot for about thirty minutes and had
an audience that was with me all the way. Then I introduced Miss
Rand. She did her act and, in closing, stepped to the microphone
and asked: "What part of the show did you like best?" A dozen
clowns in that audience shouted "Bill Sands."

As soon as I had closed the show, I hurried backstage to Miss
Rand's dressing room.

"I'm sorry for what happened," I began unhappily. "But I was
only trying to do my best and . . ."

"Don't you worry about it, Bill," she interrupted calmly. "Sally
Rand has never in her life asked an entertainer to cut his act or
water it down so that she could close the show. These people came
here to see both of us perform. They're entitled to our best. Don't
you ever give them less. And don't worry about me. I'll get along just
fine."

She always has and she always will.

My world was warm, gratifying and exciting. Sometimes it was funny.

There was the time I was sitting with Paul Gilbert, a motion picture actor who formerly starred in the Colgate Comedy Hour. We were discussing the difficulties a comedian faces during the first few minutes on the stage. Paul said: "How would you like to have an opening that will, without fail, get your audience 100 percent attentive in the first thirty seconds?"

"I'd love it. So would everyone else in the business."

"Well," said Paul, "I'll give you such an opening. Free. No strings attached. I'll guarantee it will get the wholehearted attention of the house within thirty seconds."

"What is it?" I asked.

"Watch me tonight at the Crescendo," he answered. "I'll save you a ringside seat."

I was there when the band struck up Paul's walk-on music.

"Good evening, ladies and gentlemen. It's good to be back in Hollywood," he began. "It's good to be here, if for no other reason than the fact it gives me the opportunity to visit my psychiatrist again."

"Oh, no. . . ." I thought.

"Yep," said Paul to the audience. "I saw my psychiatrist today. When he finished examining me, I asked him 'How am I doing, Doc?' The doctor said, 'Paul, you are cured. . . .'"

"Cured?" Paul shouted at the audience. "I flipped." Whereupon, with no warning and no perceptible change in stance, Paul launched himself straight up in the air into a forward layout somersault. It seemed as if he hung five feet in the air for an eternity—he was higher than the top of the microphone—stretched straight out with his back parallel to the floor. And then he came down. Straight down.

He landed on that stage with a bone-cracking jolt. The audience was stunned. So, I assumed was Paul. Stunned, if not dead. Before the burst of applause came, however, as he lay there, he turned his head and winked at me, "That's it. You can have it."

"Thanks," I said dryly. "What would I do for an encore?"

Afterwards I found out Paul Gilbert had been a "high flyer" for the Ringling Brothers Circus, had performed on the high wire and the horizontal bar, as a tumbler and had done a hand-balancing act.

The memories I treasure most, however, far beyond any reputation I made for myself, include the beautiful ballad "What's the Good in Good Night" ("When I'm Saying Good Night to You") that Jack LeDell composed. A graduate of Julliard School of Music, Jack has a degree in nearly every instrument in the band. He gave me this lovely song, without strings, simply because he thought it would improve my act.

There was Helen Boice, a red-hot momma type, whose heart is as big as her hefty, but graceful body. She gave me her arrangements of "Mañana" and "A Good Man Is Hard to Find." Not only did she hand them to me, she even donated her time in rehearsing me to be sure they were effective. They were.

There was Norm Hagee, a bandleader in Seattle, known to be an absolute stickler for demanding that acts furnish him exact arrangements, with full parts for each of his musicians. He would not tolerate half-baked "talk-over" rehearsals. Everything had to be precise and fully rehearsed. Yet this man gave unstintingly of his time and his invaluable knowledge when all my arrangements were stolen from my parked car. (Perhaps it was a form of poetic justice that I, a former bandit, suffered this irreparable loss.) Norm turned out a beautiful and highly complex arrangement when I walked on that night. There was the friendship of Blanche Cooper of the Cooper Sisters, and her constructive criticism of my work; and Kitt Carson, whose figure is a death warrant to those girls who think they have cleavage. There was the generous friendship of Billy Daniels and his accompanist, Benny Payne. And the little strippers, who often shared one dressing room with me as if it were a dormitory.

I had heard the rumors of sexual immorality among show people. But either I walked through those years in a total daze or the stories are lies. The show people I knew led their own lives and allowed me the dignity of mine. It was usually some nut from the audience who made indecent advances or propositions.

This was a good time of life for me. I was delighted to be able to help people forget their troubles, even if only briefly. But it wasn't enough to satisfy the ache deep within me. I couldn't imagine it would ever be enough.

Thus I rushed from one interest to another. Racing came next. I bought a sports car. A friend of mine took me to his sports car club one evening, and there I met about fifty young men, most of them sports car owners. They seemed to collect a vast number of trick gadgets—imported driving gloves, berets with pompoms, metal badges of foreign derivation. They were watching a color motion picture of a *Grand Prix* race in Europe. Like them, I was fascinated by the incredible speed of the drivers, the beautifully executed turns and the approach to the checkered flag. When it was over, the members cheered and applauded. There was a good deal of handshaking and backslapping. Then they all took off in a great roar of engines and straight pipe mufflers.

"Did you have a good time?" asked my friend.

It was interesting, I said, and asked if the club had any races scheduled. Apparently not—so I scouted around to find out where there would be some actual racing. I drove down to chat with members of the entry committee and to find out the requirements. I would need seat belts and a helmet (this was before roll bars were required) I was informed, then I would be allowed to enter the Pismo Beach Hill Climb. This was to be a dirt track road test to discover how fast a car could climb a sharply rising narrow road marked by hairpin turns and fast bends. I entered, without having any modifications made on the engine of my car. Here again, my need to meet challenge was of tremendous help; I came out class winner.

During the following year I met some of the sports car racing drivers of America, among them Ken Miles and Phil Hill. I also saw some of the finest racing machinery in the world, the $18,000 and up Ferraris, the little Alfa-Romeos, the Porsches. My own MG fell into one of the lowest classes of engine displacement.

I was hooked.

I learned by experience that smoothness equals speed. While it may look daring to get a car into a wild skid, such maneuvers cost the driver vital time and may lose a race for him. It is the smooth driver taking the same turn with scarcely a lean or a squeal who usually wins.

Road racing, to me, required the same kind of survival reaction as had San Quentin. You took your one opening, the first time it presented itself. Your timing, your speed, what your car would do, everything had to be calculated at once, and it had to work, now. There was no second chance.

Reflexes alone were not enough. It required judgment, know-how, knowledge of your machine, knowledge of yourself—the optimum performance of both driver and car. And over and over again—smoothness was emphasized to me.

That year I raced in a number of events, usually winning my class, sometimes placing overall, and invariably finding excitement and fascination. Most of my money went into machinery of various kinds for my racing. Among the nineteen automobiles I owned and raced that year were: an Allard with a Cadillac engine in it, which blew everything in its class off the road at Palm Springs; a 145-mile-per-hour Aston Martin; a Jowet Jupiter of brilliant emerald-green classic lines, but comparatively little power; a racing Ferrari, which I was not allowed to drive on the streets; a Porsche, and a Simca.

During this period I also tried out a motorcycle. In competent hands a motorcycle can be taken on trails at high speeds. I thoroughly enjoyed the 2-wheel hill climbs and took quite a few spills before I mastered the art of jumping motorcycles and of power-riding these skittish mounts on one wheel.

As a challenge to our skills, three other men and I decided to traverse the wilderness area of the high Sierras between Fresno, California, and the Nevada state line. Our attempt was written up in a national motorcycle magazine under the title, "They Said It Couldn't Be Done—and It Couldn't." It took us three days in all, and we finally walked into a ranger station, half-frozen in our summer shirts, after a 2-day trek, without food and over a snow field. We had lost our bikes over cliffs and in rivers.

What was there to attempt after this but flying? I chose as my instruction base a *fly or die* airport at Boulder, Colorado. The airstrip seemed the size of a postage stamp. On one side towered the formidable Rocky Mountain peaks; on the other, there was a drop of some one thousand feet into oblivion.

I received my pilot's license and began piling up hours. Later, in order to spend as much time as possible in the air, I started an aerial photography business. It didn't earn much for me, but I was in it for the thrill of flying. I'd practice my 720's, pulling my little single engine through its own prop wash, and other maneuvers. I also enjoyed making unorthodox practice landings against the time when I might have to make an emergency landing. The day I began my first growth of grey hair came when I had to fly from Boulder to Pueblo to compete in a road race. It was a 2-driver event. A young novice driver, who showed a lot of promise, and I were to drive an MG in a 2-hour race. He was at the other end, waiting for me, but the day in Boulder dawned foggy, with clouds hanging well below my high-altitude airport.

When I arrived at the Boulder airport, the owner, who had also been my flying instructor, told me it was impossible to take off.

"Look," I answered, "I have nearly a hundred hours in this airplane, and I know whether I can fly it or not."

"You know more about flying now," he said sarcastically, "than you will when you have a thousand hours." Now that my hours have piled up, I know what he said was true.

I reasoned that since I was flying an Ercoupe, a small 2-place, single-engined plane that had no rudder pedals (advertisements said you "fly it like you drive a car") and because I had a compass, altimeter, air-speed indicator and rate-of-climb meter, I had a good chance to make it.

"This plane can't spin—you taught me that," I said. "All I need to do is to take off, fly east from the Rocky Mountains, maintain a steady rate of climb and I'll be out of this soup."

"That may be so," he said, "but you won't be able to do it. You need a turn-and-bank indicator. Vertigo will get you. You need a gyrocompass instead of your magnetic."

What he did not explain was that although my reasoning was sound—provided I had the right instruments—there is a lag in the magnetic compass that ruins its use for instrument flying. A sudden updraft or downdraft, will buffet a plane as much as ninety degrees off course. Because of the lag in the compass, it is impossible to correct before another buffet of wind compounds the error.

Vertigo meant nothing to me. Not then. I took off. Visibility was limited to about a hundred feet. In practically no time I had lost sight of the ground. I was in a grey world with mists that swirled with sickening speed past my wing tips.

For a short while everything went as I had anticipated. For perhaps three or four minutes I flew steadily east at a climb-out speed of ninety miles an hour. My altimeter told me I was climbing through the soup and should break out into the clear.

Then it happened. Everything seemed to stand still, everything except the compass. It suddenly showed I was headed due west, right into the Rocky Mountains. I executed a turn and corrected for it. But now the compass was spinning wildly. The wing tips gave me no point of reference. Everything was grey and motionless. *Either the compass is crazy or I am,* I thought, trying desperately to steer in any direction. I was getting sick. Then my air speed started to drop. Loss of air speed is the most dangerous thing of all in an airplane; it means a stall and, inevitably, a crash. I looked out at the leading edge of the wing. The wings were icing and ice was blocking the opening to the air-speed indicator.

I struggled desperately to gain altitude above the clouds. Many times I felt the telltale shudder that comes just before a stall, and I could not be sure whether I was right-side up, sideways or upside down. Perspiration rolled down the inside of my shirt; I could feel it sticking my pants to the seat. Sweat stung my eyes and made my hands slippery on the wheel.

"Don't panic," I said aloud, "or you'll sure find a cloud with a rock in it."

Then I saw the sun. But it was a crazy sun that crossed the dome of my little airplane from horizon to horizon, starting on one wing tip and disappearing underneath the other. My senses told me the sun had gone crazy, but my intellect told me it was my airplane describing that peculiar maneuver. A couple more of those sun streaks and I managed to right the plane above the clouds, then headed south toward my road race. When I landed at the airport at Pueblo, I was a better pilot because I had found out the hard way how little I knew.

That was the only time a road race seemed anticlimactic. The records of the Pike's Peak Sports Car Club, sponsors of the race, show that at the end of forty-five minutes of driving, I had completely lapped every other car in my class and some of those in the classes above mine. Jerry and I won, but I didn't even stay for the trophy dinner. For once in my life, I'd had all the excitement I wanted in one day.

To some it may have appeared like a waste of time. But to me it was a search—by this time a conscious one—for something that would satisfy me.

Still, if it weren't speed or danger or faraway places or excitement, what was "it?" That "it" I was after sometimes seemed on the verge of showing itself to me. Then the veil obscuring it would seem to be securely drawn.

Adventure was not the answer.

11

I WAS IN DALLAS FOR A COUPLE OF SHOW dates in the summer of 1960, and it struck me as a good place to live. It was two years after I had resigned from Silhouette to rest and spend the money I had accumulated—which I did in Europe for a year. A big state, Texas, with room for big ideas. I placed an ad in the newspaper, looking for a position as a sales executive.

One answer came from a man who had the germ of a good idea but lacked know-how to put it together. Simply stated, it was a plan whereby, with an expenditure of only $1,000, a parent could assure his child of an adequately financed college education. If, for some reason, the child did not attend college, the parent would get the $1,000 back.

The basic premise was simple. By combining two heretofore unrelated statistics—the school dropout records furnished by the United States Department of Health, Education and Welfare, and the compound interest statistics furnished by the Federal Deposit Insurance Corporation—the idea became a workable plan.

If a number of parents would deposit $1,000 in a federally insured savings account, with the understanding that the interest accruing to those accounts would be used for the education of those children who survived the dropout statistics, then, actuarial figures proved, each college student would have enough money to finance a college education. In other words, the interest forfeited by the children who did not go to college, or by parents who cancelled the plan by withdrawing their $1,000, paid for the college education of those children who did continue. Children enrolled in this plan for twelve years or more prior to college age would have at least $5,000 for their college education. The premise of the plan was simple. The details, however, proved to be complex. A hundred questions immediately came to mind. How old must the child be? Who distributes the monies? What if my child dies? Who pays for the upkeep and bookkeeping of the plan? What if my child doesn't finish college? I hired a Dallas attorney of outstanding reputation, a certified public accountant, a former judge who was also a member of the Texas State Legislature, an insurance actuary and business advisors. Ultimately, we were able to answer every question to the satisfaction of everyone concerned, including officials of the State of Texas.

It was decided to charge a nonrefundable enrollment fee of $100 in order to finance commissions, auditing costs, advertising, administrative expenses and profit for the organizers. Thus, the trust fund money would not have to be touched. Every cent of interest would go toward the education of children. When everything had been figured out, there was a profit of $20 per enrollment for the organizers of the plan.

To set up this plan took money. I used all of my own, then borrowed some and, finally, took in a partner. At last we were ready with everything in written form, including sales books, advertising, brochures, articles of incorporation for the scholarship fund, articles of incorporation for a second and separate corporate structure to handle the $100 enrollment fees. It was submitted to the State attorney general's office for approval and came back almost immediately, along with the two charters from the corporation commissioner. We were practically in business.

A Federal Reserve bank was selected and approved, and although every legal advisor had informed us the entire plan was strictly a banking function, we voluntarily decided to place all of the employees, as well as the plan itself, under the scrutiny of the Texas State Securities Commission. We submitted everything to them, and my attorney said the securities commissioner had informed him, verbally, that a securities license was required simply for "form and screening personnel."

Field testing seemed the only thing remaining before putting it into operation. I telephoned the two best sales executives I knew to join me in this. (I knew them from the reducing business.)

The tests succeeded beyond our wildest hopes. More than 90 percent of the parents whom we approached wanted to enroll their children immediately. All we needed now was the green light from our attorney to start hiring our sales personnel.

To supplement my waning income I was making appearances in nightclubs. As a result, Tony Zoppi, a Dallas newspaper columnist, invited me to appear on his television show, "Dallas After Dark." This was a real break for me as his widely viewed program had featured such stars as Frank Sinatra, Dean Martin, Diana Dors and Sammy Davis, Jr. in the weeks immediately preceding.

Zoppi usually conducted a short interview with his guests before they did their act. In introducing me he said, "Bill has been a race car driver, a professional prize fighter, a pilot, a championship water-skier and a water-polo player; he led a diamond expedition into the unexplored jungles of Venezuela, and coached Florence Chadwick for her English Channel swim. Gee, Bill, have I left anything out?"

"Yes, Tony," I said, with no thought at all about my next words, "I am also an ex-convict. I was in San Quentin Prison more than two years, and most of that time I was a cell mate of Caryl Chessman."

It was out, and Tony made the most of it. If it were not for the video tape made of the show, I could not tell to this day what I said. With Tony's encouragement, I capsulized my life story. I heard myself telling my views about Chessman, who had been executed three months before; about juvenile delinquency; about capital punishment. The band never struck up my cue. The musicians had crept forward to listen to us. When the program was over and I realized it had gone in such an unscheduled manner, I offered to redo it. But Tony said, "It will be great and will really wake people up." His prognostication was accurate. Reaction was widespread and favorable. Tony told me, "Your appearance has drawn more mail than any program I have given so far, and letters are still coming in. I want you back and soon."

Certainly I could use some good news, as the scholarship plan seemed to be hitting one snag after the other in the labyrinth of the securities commission scrutiny. In spite of the meticulous care that had been exercised from start to finish in setting up the plan and selecting personnel, it appeared to me that the plan was being stalled.

As the result of the Tony Zoppi show, however, I was put in touch with a West Coast magazine writer who wanted to discuss my life story for possible use in magazine or book form. After several telephone conversations, I agreed to meet him in Los Angeles, although the scholarship plan could ill spare me at the moment. My attorney saw me off at the plane and promised to keep in touch by telephone.

The interview in Los Angeles had been going eight hours a day on a tape recorder for several days when the magazine writer asked me the nature of my business in Dallas. With his quick mind, he had no difficulty in understanding its potential, including the tremendous money-making possibilities. He said it gave him an idea for an additional story, "Texas Has the Answer." More than that, he wanted in. Because of his reputation, I appointed him our director of public relations. He called the idea a "stroke of financial genius," and became its ardent advocate. As a matter of fact, he seemed to forget the original purpose for summoning me to Los Angeles.

Meanwhile, he told me there was someone he wanted me to meet. This was the woman reporter, Eleanor Garner Black, who had covered Chessman's execution—the first woman to see a death penalty carried out in California. I had no desire to talk with any hard-boiled reporter who had watched my friend die, and I said so.

"But I think you can help her," he said.

"Why the hell should I want to? And what kind of help does she need, anyway?"

"Well," the writer said slowly, "she believed in his innocence. She liked him and she didn't think it was a death penalty crime in any event. . . ."

"Then why did she go and watch him die?" I asked indignantly.

"You will have to ask her that," he told me. "Newspaper reporters go where they are sent. There is just as much of 'the show must go on' tradition among the press as in show business. But she hasn't been the same since. I talked to her on the telephone the other day and she told me she has been asked to write her views on the Chessman case for a symposium being gathered by a noted criminologist. She says she can no longer write about it. After she did her story on the execution she apparently built a mental block around it. Now she's faced with a real dilemma—if a writer can't write, what is there left? Perhaps you might help her. I do wish you would see her."

"Okay." I gave in. "Make a date for dinner with her."

"I already have," he announced. "Tonight."

But the woman who opened the door of the little house in Glendora was not prepared to go out. She was dressed in slacks and a plain white blouse, and her red hair was done in a ponytail. Her face, devoid of makeup, was not beautiful, but it was interesting and attractive. Her manner, however, was cool. Standing with her in the doorway was a small, curious child. The woman invited us in, then excused herself while she took the little girl to the back of the house.

"I think I've met her before," I said to my writer friend.

"Well, it's possible," he answered. "She's been a newspaper reporter for nearly eighteen years, and she might have covered one or more of your didoes."

"I don't mean that. I just have the curious feeling that I know her well."

As she busied herself pouring coffee a few minutes later I studied her intently. She was short, about five-feet-two, but it was obvious that under the slacks and blouse was a beautifully compact, athletic, but feminine figure.

"I hope you will excuse my not being ready to go out," she said, "but I just don't feel up to talking about Caryl Chessman at dinner.

In fact I don't feel much like talking about him at all. But I suppose if anyone has the right to inquire, it's you. I understand you were once his cellmate."

"That's right," I said, hoping to make her feel more at ease. "We met when we were both first offenders. Chess and I were cell mates and spent our working hours together. We were close friends."

"I expected you to look different, somehow," the woman said.

"In what way?"

"Oh, I don't know. Our friend here told me you were some kind of clerk in San Quentin, and I guess I expected you to look more like a clerk and less like—well, an athlete maybe?" She smiled. This was the first friendly overture she had made.

"If you don't mind—if you feel up to it—I would like to hear from you about Chessman. About the way he was when he died."

She rose quickly trotted into another part of the house, came back with a newspaper in her hand. She shoved this under my nose, and then slapped it with the back of her hand imperiously.

"If there's anything you want to know about Chessman's death, read it," she commanded. "I didn't spare a detail." With that she sat down across the room from me, arms folded belligerently, staring at me with narrowed eyes. For a moment she reminded me of myself, the way I used to be almost twenty years before.

"I have read it," I said quietly, folding the newspaper. "I didn't ask you what killed him. I know. He was executed in the gas chamber. What I asked, was how he was when he died. I don't mean the gory details of an execution, but what kind of a man he was. . . ."

"I don't know how he was when you knew him." Her eyes were focused on something way beyond the living room. "He may have been violent and detestable and all the things they say—I only knew him for the last three years before he died—and on the day he died. If they had killed him before, when he was a young gunman, I suppose there would have been little loss. But the man they killed last May was the wrong man. He was incapable of sex crimes. He was a good person, totally rehabilitated—much less violent and hostile about things than I am right now."

The pent-up words came slowly at first, then in a rush. As she spoke of Chessman's personality and the many ramifications of his legal case, I could see she not only had a thorough understanding of criminal law, but that she had also been close to him.

"You say he was rehabilitated. How do you know?" I persisted gently.

"Because I am rehabilitated myself—or at least I am in the process." This woman was full of surprises. And I would have to know her for a long time to know her really well.

"You—and Chess—showed your defiance and hostility in one way. I might have shown mine in the same way had I been a man. As it is I showed my defiance by taking to the bottle." Her wide-set jade-green eyes showed a spark of remembered rebellion.

"When I was about 18, I had completed four years of the most intensive swimming training. I had qualified for the 1940 Olympic team, but we didn't get to go. The games were scheduled to be held in Finland and, if you recall, Finland was invaded by the Russians that year."

How well I recalled.

"Because of my training I was in very good shape when I began to drink with some of my newspaper cronies. I could hold liquor well and the people I drank with gave me the idea this was something to be proud of." She smiled, shaking her head ruefully.

"Drinking seemed to cushion the disillusionments one experiences in the early days of reporting. Finally, after a great deal of drinking and a great deal of trouble, including an arrest for drunk driving, I decided to do something about it."

Her frankness amazed me. "When I decided to stop drinking, it was not merely a case of going on the wagon. It was a lifetime program. I had to find some kind of moral or spiritual help. I did. I have not had a drink in eight years, and I doubt if I will ever have another. . . ."

At this point, unexpectedly, my writer friend interrupted: "Now, Pony," he addressed her by her nickname, "you don't really believe you were an alcoholic, do you?"

"Well, if I wasn't, I would do until one came along." She was looking at me. "That'd be like saying you really didn't mean it when you stuck a gun in somebody's face and relieved him of his money. Of course, you meant it and were daring anyone to take your fun away from you, isn't that so?" Without waiting for an answer, she plunged on. "Well, I meant it, too. So did Chessman. So does anyone who deliberately violates the law. But when that same person makes a turnabout—you no longer rob, and I no longer drink—I believe it should be taken just as seriously by those who are involved and by others who insist upon having opinions about it. People, such as our friend here, are too prone to discount either the good or the bad as being unreal."

This was fascinating to me. I had met a number of women who "forgave" me my criminal past, but none who understood that one man, in one lifetime, could be both very good and very bad. At last I had met a woman who understood what rehabilitation really is.

Our conversation covered many subjects and, eventually, she answered all my questions about Chessman's last days. She related facts I would have had no other way of learning. To gauge her reaction, I told her about the scholarship plan. For I had noticed over the past several weeks that the plan served, in the telling, as an absolute greed index. The people with me in Dallas had seized upon it, immediately, as a great benefit to children. Others were quick to recognize its tremendous money-making potential. This latter reaction was true of the magazine writer. But Pony exclaimed instantly, "What a wonderful idea. Do you realize the federal and local governments have been beating their brains out for years trying to figure out some way to help more children afford college. There is also the matter of juvenile delinquency—a kid brought up from the first grade with the idea that he is destined for college seldom winds up as a delinquent. . . ."

Her reaction to the plan told me several things about her that I wanted to know. When we left, well past midnight, I could not concentrate on the writer's usually stimulating conversation. My mind was back in her little house. I wondered why she seemed so familiar to me. From our conversation about the schools we had attended (she was only months younger than I) I knew we could not possibly have met then. Still . . .

When we arrived at the writer's home, the telephone was ringing. It was Dallas. My attorney had been trying to get me for hours. The securities commission still had not acted, he said, and he thought I had better return as soon as possible. I told the writer about developments, and together we went over every phase of the plan, from its inception to its present status.

"There's absolutely nothing wrong with it," he said. "It's a fine plan. It's workable. But do you realize it would strike a terrific blow at the educational endowment plans offered by some insurance companies? Is there an insurance lobby in Texas?"

That was an entirely new consideration for me. I had little sleep that night and prepared to leave in the morning. I telephoned Pony to ask her to go to the airport with me. "I want to see you again— just as a friend, and not to talk about Chess."

"Okay," she said. "Stop by the paper on your way."

When the writer and I picked her up, her appearance was in sharp contrast to what it had been the other evening. She was well-dressed, well-groomed, vivacious. Then, all too quickly, they were seeing me off. Loath to end Pony's happy conversation, I invited her, on an impulse, to accompany me back to Dallas. I meant it. And she knew it.

"On occasions, I have pulled some fast ones on my baby-sitter," she bantered. "But those were unintentional. I don't see how I could explain an unintentional trip to Dallas."

"I only wanted to continue our conversation," I said truthfully. "I would put you on the next plane back to Los Angeles. Our visit seems so chopped-off this way. . . ."

"It really does seem like a sudden ending, doesn't it?" We were walking from the ticket counter, down the ramp, to the boarding gate, when she added, "You told me you were in show business and now, just think, you have to leave without my seeing your act. . . ."

Whereupon, with a lack of inhibition I had neither exhibited nor felt in years, I accommodated her by bursting into a medley of Al Jolson songs. We ignored the startled glances and whisperings of passersby. The writer, who had driven us to the airport, was completely forgotten. The impromptu entertainment ended with a rendition of "Mammy," with me on one knee at the boarding gate while my ticket was being checked. A flash of her press pass allowed Pony to accompany me through the gate and to the plane. There, dropping all pretense of humor, I said. "I'm going to see you again. Either you are coming to Texas—you and your little girl—or I am coming back to Los Angeles. I'll telephone you—tonight."

12

My ATTORNEY AND MY TOP STAFF GREETED me at Love Field with tales of troubles that had beset them and the scholarship plan during my 9-day absence.

The complaints were valid. The securities commission was now insisting upon a verbatim repetition of every single word that was in the instruction and training of my sales force. These instructions, of course, had not been recorded for posterity, and I was the only one who could supply the information. By morning, there were additional problems, all requiring my attention. My attorney was at a loss to explain what was happening. He decided to go to Austin to see. At that time, the former judge, now a member of the Texas State Legislature, came into the picture; he was a friend of my attorney. He volunteered to drive to Austin, where he was well known. He was confident he could resolve the delays or at least discover the reason for them.

While he was away, I had my hands full with other matters, mostly Pony. I called her each night, certain that in her I'd find a sympathetic and intelligent confidante. After leaving Los Angeles, it seemed to me as if Pony and I were being held apart—that actually we had always been together and this separation was new. I couldn't find words to describe it, but I didn't like it.

Meanwhile, in the office there were forty fully trained topnotch sales people, who on my say-so had given up jobs to come and work for me—and for more than three weeks had not been permitted to earn a living. They were "solid" in the finest meaning of that word. Daily, they expressed faith in me, in the scholarship plan and in the eventual happy outcome.

Friday, four days after he left for Austin, the judge returned and gave us the good news.

"Everything has finally been cleared," he said. "You have the official go-ahead to start selling. The license will be forthcoming at the beginning of the week. Good luck."

My salesmen swarmed out; I, of course, telephoned Pony. It looked as if all the hard work and meticulous care were about to pay off. It was a happy staff that poured in for the Monday sales meeting. During that first weekend more than $400,000 in scholarship plans had been sold. Each man had averaged $300 or more for himself in immediate commission income. My personal profit, after all expenses and other deductions, was just under $20,000. Never was there less need for any sort of pep talk from a sales manager to his staff.

It was into this happy hubbub that the judge came. Everyone applauded.

"I have some bad news for you," he said solemnly. "We have been unofficially served with a 'cease and desist' order. I don't understand it. Neither does my contact in Austin. I'm taking the next plane down to the capital to get the answer. Meanwhile, no more scholarships can be sold. If any attempt is made to do so, people are going to wind up in jail. It's only because I'm a member of the Legislature that I was given the courtesy of a telephone call first. Once I find out something, I will be on the telephone. Meanwhile, let's all hope for good news."

"If this 'cease and desist' order has come as a result of our not having the securities license actually in a frame on the wall here, I hope you recall that it was you who made the announcement and told these people to go to work," I protested.

"I know it," he replied calmly, "but I had been given the absolute word by some of my friends in the capital. I have known these men for years and have no reason to doubt them. I feel sure there is some explanation."

"It will take more than an explanation to satisfy my people." I was fiercely indignant at the obvious "politicking" behind the scenes. "This time it will take the license. The license for which we have filled every requirement ten times over."

"I intend to get it," the judge said, as he hurried away.

I could not reach Pony on the telephone, so I called our magazine-writer friend. Before I could tell him what had happened in Dallas, he told me he had talked to one of the editors of the *Saturday Evening Post*, and this man was "hot for the story." When I told him tersely what had transpired, he said: "Go ahead with it anyway. Nothing's wrong with that plan. I've examined it from every angle. So has my attorney. It's not only perfectly legal, but highly moral and necessary. Send your salesmen out. We can, if necessary, have it tried in the newspapers. Public opinion will overwhelm local politicking. Your plan will succeed. Politicians have a way of feeling the public pulse. They'll never oppose a plan that meets with good public reaction."

Just then the former judge called from Austin on another telephone. "Bill, they have found out, down here, that you have a felony record."

"Found out!" I exploded. "Well, that was damn clever of them considering that I've been on television with it and in Tony Zoppi's newspaper column, and that everyone here knows. . . ."

"Anyway," he interrupted, "that's the explanation. The securities commission won't grant your license. That is, it won't grant a license for the scholarship plan unless you are out of it. They want you to resign. That's not all. All the money you've taken in so far is to be refunded. They won't be content with just a resignation. They want you to get rid of your stock."

"But what have I done?" I demanded.

"You are an ex-convict," he replied.

"That in itself means I have been punished, nothing else."

"I know, but . . ."

"Is that the entire story?" I asked.

"That's it," he told me tersely.

"You mean they are going to stop this scholarship plan, prevent thousands of kids from getting a college education because twenty years ago, when I was under age, I committed a felony and was punished for it? You know that I have been out of prison for eighteen years and my parole was discharged about fifteen years ago. Do they know that?"

"Yes, they know all that. But they say the scholarship plan cannot go into effect with you in it." His voice was low, but final. "I'll see you as soon as I get back to Dallas."

By the time I talked to Pony, I saw my clear choice. On one hand, I could follow the writer's well-intentioned advice and stay with it. By blackjacking the legislators, the scholarship plan would succeed, be a great benefit to a lot of youngsters and I could make a lot of money. But it would involve bending my ethics. On the other hand, I could withdraw. Pony's reaction was instantaneous—and it was similar to mine.

"Don't surrender any ethics now," she said, her voice breaking a little. "Obviously it is politics—your being an ex-convict is merely an excuse. But you've never done a legally or morally questionable thing since you have come out of San Quentin. Why start? I do have another thought, however. Every inventor gets a small percentage, a royalty. Couldn't you ask for some kind of agreement so you could share in the profits?"

Eventually, that was what I sought. With the partner I had taken in, I signed a royalty agreement, transferred all of my stock to him and had my name removed from all of the papers. To say it was a blow would be an understatement. I had learned people don't die just because they sometimes feel as if they would like to. I was tasting for the first time defeat, complete defeat. My mother's beatings hadn't been able to do it, nor my father's death, nor San Quentin, nor sharks nor jungle cats.

But it happened in Dallas.

I made an attempt to look forward. There was my life story now in the hands of the magazine writer. There was, thank God, Pony. I shook the dust of Dallas from my feet.

"The inevitable implosion." It was Pony with her arms around my neck. "I felt as if we were being forced apart like a split atom," she whispered, out of breath in my vise-like grip, "and this is the implosion."

So she felt about us as I did.

At her house I became acquainted with her daughter, an enchanting child, full of energy and curiosity. The following day we went to Pacific Ocean Park where 6-year-old Bonnie led us a merry chase. That night, while she was in the care of a baby-sitter, I took her mother to a quiet restaurant.

"I want to talk seriously," I said as soon as we were seated and the waiter had taken our order. "As far as I am concerned, our relationship has deepened into something more than friendship."

"Yes, I know."

"Well, here are several things you ought to know. Since meeting you I've had you under a mental microscope. I've tried to figure out not only your thoughts, but the concepts responsible for them. I've wanted to know your actions and reactions, your hopes and dreams and fears. I think I know you—the real you—more intimately than you could possibly suspect. Now it's time for you to know something about me."

"I already do."

"No," I interrupted. "You are not aware of what I want to say now. May I say it?"

"Certainly."

"I'll break every rule of salesmanship by starting with the punch line first. I want you to marry me. Now, don't interrupt, because there's more to it than that. You see, when I was in San Quentin some things happened to me. . . ."

I opened my soul and poured out the heartbreak of the lonely days, weeks, months and years in prison, when no one really cared about me—loved me—or, more important, needed me.

I explained how I had dreamed of a woman who could make me happy. A woman who would know how those days had affected me— how they affected me still. A woman who would have firsthand knowledge of rehabilitation. A lifetime partner from whom no secrets would be kept; a mate with whom I could share everything.

"You," I said, "are that woman. That was why when we first met, I was sure I knew you. I dreamed of you, your complete character, but I hadn't seen you! But you should know I've made a great many mistakes. It seems as though I have to learn the hard way—by experience. I should have been content forever with some of the jobs I've had, yet I couldn't be. I'm restless—I still haven't identified much that I'm looking for or hoping to be. So you see, I'm no bargain. I hope this has nothing to do with us, but I had to tell you."

"I understand," said Pony, softly.

"At San Quentin, I grew a protective shell," I said. "I didn't think it would ever be cracked. Until now. But I need to be needed.

"During those dark days, I resolved that never again as long as I lived would I put myself in a position to be hurt, the way I had been when I realized that even my own mother neither loved nor needed me. That resolve has grown stronger, until now it is basic to my personality. I think you need me. I know I need you. If you need me enough—if I can somehow know that you would never let me down, no matter what the circumstances—then I believe that shell of mine could be destroyed.

"I am complex in many ways. As I've already told you, I have yet to find my place in life. Nothing I have undertaken, no matter how exciting or successful, has ever given me any real satisfaction. That, too, I believe, we could somehow achieve together.

"Last, but not least, is the fact that since my release from San Quentin Prison, I have never intentionally done a dishonest or immoral act or anything to hurt my fellow man. I have made many mistakes, however, or I would be better situated today."

"You don't have to tell me the kind of life you have led since San Quentin," answered Pony. "Don't you give me credit for any insight?"

"The gallant thing to do," I said, "is to give you time to think it over. So, I'll give you all of the time you want—between now and the moment the waiter pours our next cup of coffee."

Pony's answer was direct. "I've had my struggles, too. My chief battles, like yours, have been with myself. I've had to learn some things the hard way too. We had quite a bit of money when I was a kid—I had many advantages. But we lost everything in the Depression. Then later I had to go to work after a year of college. More recently I was the sole support of my marriage—I was glad I was able. Other difficulties came up and I got a divorce. Some of the men in my profession challenged my right to be there and made things rough for me. But at least I learned some valuable lessons along the way. Perhaps some of my hard-won insights could be of help to you—and I know you could help me."

After dinner, I took Pony to meet my friend, Jim. I related how he and I had met and what had happened to him in the intervening years.

"Jim became county superintendent at Arrowhead after I went to Arabia. I kept in touch with him by letter. He kept me posted on Chessman's legal battle and sent me clippings from the newspapers.

"About eight years ago, when I returned to the States, I found Jim in a veterans' hospital. He had cancer of the throat and a fifty-fifty chance of living through an operation. He made it all right, but his larynx and his vocal cords were removed. I found him lying in his hospital bed with a slate for communication.

"For a man so well read, who enjoyed the art of conversation, this was a hideous tragedy. While I was there, a psychiatrist brought a visitor—a man who had undergone the same operation. This fellow could speak, but in a hesitant voice that had no tone. What he did really was to belch forth a word or two at a time. This was done by gathering air into the stomach and then expelling it while shaping a word with his mouth.

" 'Some . . . day . . .' he told Jim, 'you . . . will . . . talk . . . like . . . this.'

"After his visitor left, Jim grabbed the slate and scribbled furiously, 'I'll never talk like that.' The doctor tried to calm him. 'It takes time, but some day you will talk again.' Whereupon Jim wrote with emphasis, 'I didn't say I'd never talk. I said I'd never talk *like that.*'

"Well, they let him go home for Christmas. I had just arrived, and his wife and I were so happy he was alive, we didn't care whether he talked or not. But how he cared. Each time I asked him something, the talk would bog down while he wrote a reply. We became horribly self-conscious. I framed my words so that none of them formed questions.

"Suddenly he got up, tossed the slate in the fireplace, stomped off to the bathroom, slammed the door and locked it. We waited anxiously. We both knew that one of the deepest impressions of Jim's life stemmed from his childhood memory of his grandfather. That fine old man had broken a hip at the age of eighty-five. He shot himself, leaving a note, saying 'I've gone as far as I care to go.'

"We were both shaken by the fear that Jim intended to do away with himself, but with such a strong-willed man, there was no use in trying to break down the door. It would only postpone his action. Two hours passed in tension; there had been no sound of a falling body, so we thought he was still alive.

"Suddenly the bathroom door opened and he stepped out.

" 'Merry Christmas.'

"It was Jim—talking! His voice was hoarse but perfectly understandable. He looked at our astonished faces and laughed with delight. Then, with considerable effort, he said, 'Figured if that guy could learn it in a year, it should take me two hours.'

"There was no hesitation or belching in his manner of speech. It was a deep voice, similar to the old one; the only difference was a slight hoarseness. From what I've read since, his feat should have been impossible—the medical journals said so, as did some of the outstanding medical men who later examined him.

"But impossible or not, Jim was talking, understandably, with wisdom and entertainment. Naturally, it didn't all happen that first evening—as a matter of fact, he stayed up all night to make sure he wouldn't forget how to speak again. But in a few weeks, he was the Jim of old. I was there when a doctor from the East said to him, 'You will find it impossible to pronounce words beginning with the letter H.'

"And Jim replied, 'The hell you say.'

"Once Jim had said to me, 'Whatever a man's mind can conceive, a man can achieve,' and when I reminded him that he sure put his money where his mouth was, he said, 'Anyway, I put my voice where my gullet was.'"

Pony and Jim hit it off, and later Jim took me aside and said, "Going to marry her, aren't you?" At my happy nod, he added, "Now, see that you do."

Three days later, December 3, 1960, in Las Vegas, Pony and I exchanged vows in a quiet ceremony. On our return to Los Angeles, I called my attorney in Dallas. He said, "Bill, it looks to me as if you'll have to write this one off."

I tried to take his advice. There was still my life story, I thought, my spirits lifting. Pony and I went to visit the writer that evening. He was the picture of dejection. I made a couple of overtures at conversation and finally I said, "Well, out with it. What's on your mind?"

He shook his head sadly and muttered, "That scholarship plan. It was so good. It would have made so much money. Why even the 2 percent which you gave me would have netted me $50,000 a year if . . ." His voice trailed off sadly.

"Of course, I realize it." My patience was not improving. "Now that it's over, what would you like to do? Hold memorial services?"

"I just can't get over it," he mourned. "I could have retired to Majorca and written books or just lounged in the sun—I need never have written another magazine story about 'young love.'"

"Okay," I said, deciding to turn to other topics. "How about the book you are writing on my life? How is that coming along?"

"Oh that. . . ." he mused, looking at the ceiling and then out the window. "Well, I have decided not to do it."

"What do you mean?"

"I have decided not to write the book. I can't. . . ."

"Why can't you?" I demanded.

"On account of the scholarship plan. . . ."

"What has the scholarship plan to do with it?"

"Well, if the scholarship plan had worked, it would have made a good story. . . ."

"It would have made a good story and it would have made you wealthy, too. But it did not work, and it looks as if it never will," I pointed out.

"The life story I gave to you ended with me on Majorca last year when I had rented a villa there, before I ever saw Dallas. It was all of the life I had lived up to then. You were very enthusiastic about writing it, about the ex-convict who became a county superintendent in the same state in which he was convicted, who worked for the United States Chamber of Commerce, who had so many adventures . . . documented adventures. At that time the scholarship plan had not even been thought of. Does that have anything to do with what we are talking about, namely your contract and interest in writing my life story?"

"Yes, it does," he replied, seeming to grope for words. "You see, it changes everything. . . ."

"It changes nothing," I told him, "with the possible exception of yourself. Apparently the smell of so much money has changed you. But I gave you $1,500 to start to write my story. You said you had to have it, so I borrowed it. Do you intend to keep that?"

"Well, I can't . . . I just can't. Everything is so changed. . . ."

"Then return the $1,500."

"I can't," he repeated. "I just can't write it and I don't have the $1,500. It's been spent."

It was useless. The man was in a fit of depression from which he couldn't be roused.

"Well, little man," I said, "your welching on me won't cause me to welch on the idea." But I could not maintain the level of my anger. There was too much pity mixed with it. "If the story of my life is worth writing, I'll write it. And if I need any help, that's built-in with Pony, here."

Pony had remained silent until after we were out of the house. "Where do we go from here?" she asked.

"We go on with our lives," I told her with as much enthusiasm as I could muster. "But not here. I simply feel we should go somewhere, start to live our lives and quit dwelling upon the past. I don't like the 'what might have been' atmosphere that pervades this area or, at least, pervades me when I'm here. How do you feel about it?"

" 'Whither thou goest, I will go,' " said Pony. "If it was good enough for Ruth, it's good enough for me. I'll resign my job. I am very fond of everyone on the Los Angeles *Examiner;* they have been good to me. But I'd rather go with you and do what you are doing, than hold you here because of something I am doing."

That was one of the things I liked about her best—her immediacy. It matched my feelings exactly. We drove into a filling station, procured a map of the United States and spread it on the pavement beside the car.

"I have done this before and have always managed to find something interesting and exciting and people I liked." I took a dime out of my pocket and flipped it, letting it fall on the map.

"Well," exclaimed Pony, "I have never been in Kansas City. I wonder what it's like and what we will find there."

She gathered up the map and pocketed my dime. Then my loyal and irrepressible bride looked up at me and said: "I'm sick of watching little people stick pins in you. Come on, Gulliver, let's travel."

13

WITH THE FEW HUNDRED DOLLARS WE
salvaged by selling some of our personal
possessions, I moved my new little family
into a rented house in Kansas City.

My emotions didn't mix. They clashed
and battled in an unholy war of bitterness
versus happiness. During the day I con-
centrated on exploring the facets of my
loved one's personality. We were growing
closer in thought. There were lengthy discussions of the intangible and spiritual
laws which we believed had brought us
together. Pony was fascinating.

She drove a car the way most men
wished they could. She swam and rode a

horse and shot a rifle that way, too. Her reflexes and co-ordination were extraordinary. She had traveled extensively, had been educated partly in Europe, but most important of all, we hit a mental stride together. I could even share her little daughter, who had begun to call me "Daddy." Pony was an endless source of physical, emotional and spiritual gratification to me.

But it was not enough.

Night after night, while she was asleep, I would turn and twist, too restless for sleep, aware that the tender words I had spoken to her came from a mouth filled with the taste of bitter vetch. The more I thought about what had happened in Dallas, the more frustrated I became.

What wrong step had I taken? Where had I failed? My motives, integrity, singleness of purpose had been toward one goal—to contribute. What of the sales people I had let down? What of the youngsters whose opportunity was gone? And the aspirations and dreams of their parents? Thousands of people who would have benefited had been let down. Because of me? Why?

Desperation was with me. There was no Front Gate here. No parole. No Duffy. No gas chamber, even. The only way to end this was to end all my thinking—for all time. That I'd have to do myself.

Always nagging, like an evil voice, was the thought that by following the magazine writer's advice I could have forced it through and won. I hadn't heard such a hell fiend's snickering since the clatter of my loom in the Jute Mill at San Quentin.

"Is the scholarship wound still throbbing?"

It was Pony's voice in the dark beside me. Apparently my tossing about had awakened her.

"I can't help it, honey. I'm sorry I woke you up. Go back to sleep."

"Go to hell!" said my gracious spouse, sitting up and turning on the lamp by the bed. "I thought we made a deal to share things. Give me a cigarette."

"I would have had a great deal to share with you if everything had worked. . . ." My voice quit on me as I thought of the happiness I had envisioned, happiness and success based on something worthwhile.

"Look, honey," her voice was tender, "I didn't marry the scholarship plan. I married you. I agreed to share your future with you, whatever that future might hold. We're here, we're committed. Together. For always. Now how is 'always' going to be?"

"I wish I knew, darling. I owe you the truth. It isn't just the scholarship plan; it's my whole life. What does it all mean? It should stand for something besides just a long string of adventures and misadventures. The scholarship plan was a means—a very fine means, I thought—of putting to some use a lifetime of experiences. It could have been the culmination of an otherwise rather selfish and purposeless existence." Then I opened up the remainder of my heart.

"If my life is not going to stand for anything more than a series of exciting episodes, fleeting sensations, I don't want to go on living— and I don't have to.

"Every concept I've ever formed has been violated. And I'm too damned tired to start all over again. I feel like saying to hell with the whole world and everything in it.

"I don't know where to go from here—except to die. I need help. I don't know where to get it, because I don't know what kind of help I need. Don't tell me to try prayer because I've tried it. Every night, for the past three months."

"When were you happy, really happy?" Pony asked gently.

"When I met you and knew you were you. . . ."

"Did you make much money when you had your own dance studios?" she interrupted.

It sounded like a tangential question. She was the master of the non sequitur, I thought.

"Yes, there was quite a bit of money in it, but I—"

"The reason I asked is that you always refer to it as one of the happiest times of your life. Yet, you never mentioned money." She was watching me intently.

"Well, money isn't so important to me, as you know. . . ."

"Of course, I know. But if not money, something else made it such a happy period. Sure you liked the people. But have you given any thought to what made it such a good time?"

"Chrissy and the other teachers were like kids to me, like our daughter, Bonnie. I looked out for them and—"

"And you helped them. Helped them to make more money than

ever before, to have pleasant lives and fun while working. You helped a couple and finally saw them happily married, didn't you?"

"Yes, I did."

"What about 'Interview Time with Warden Duffy'?"

"What about it?"

"You were happy then, too, weren't you? Even though you were in prison, you were happy. Why do you suppose that was?"

"Well, that was a good thing. It helped a lot of guys, and it helped Warden Duffy."

"And you were happy teaching the swimmers in Bombay, weren't you? You were happy the day you saved that sailor from drowning, too, weren't you? And Diane. You were happy you found a way to help her."

"I think I see what you're driving at. . . ."

"If I didn't know you and just heard about the things that made you really happy, and were asked to prescribe a course of action, I'd tell you simply to get where you could help people. All the time."

"That's easier said than done," I pointed out.

She was not to be diverted. "You want your life to stand for something. Right?"

"Right."

"You profess to believe in something spiritual. Has it occurred to you that perhaps all that has happened to you, all you've ever done could be put together to mean something? Did it ever enter your mind that there might be some reason for your going to San Quentin? Some useful purpose in all the adventures you've had since San Quentin? Haven't you learned something you can pass on to others?

"Bill, I've heard you tell sales people truths that you discovered out of your own mistakes and experiences. They listen to you as they wouldn't listen to anyone else. It's because you've been through the mill. You don't talk theory, you talk fact. I know you have something to say. But it should be said to a lot of people, not to just a few individuals. If you want to make your life stand for something, use it for that purpose. To help others."

"I've never really thought about it." If my words were not profound, my thoughts were. "Yes, I do have something to say. I think I could be of help in several different areas. I do have the ability to inspire salesmen, help them make money, teach them to follow the spiritual laws of success.

"And I also know the anatomy of rehabilitation. I know what it takes for a man to stay out of prison once he gets out. In fact, I have a lot of things I could say to parents and teachers that would help prevent people from going to prison in the first place. You're damned right I have something say."

"Now, we're getting someplace." Pony had bounced out of bed, donned my bathrobe and begun to pace the floor. Now she waved a half-empty sleeve at me.

"I've known it since the beginning. I'm only amazed that it hasn't come to you before this. I've listened to you try to make each of your adventures stand by itself and, as you say, it comes to nothing more than a series of exciting episodes.

"You've been trying to deny your past. You've been running. You started running when you left your mother, and you ran all the way into San Quentin. And after San Quentin you kept right on running; each time you had a new adventure, you had something else to run from. Now you're running from your whole life. Running from it instead of toward it. It's like trying to run from your shadow. You just can't run fast enough to get away from it."

"You know something, honey—" I reached out and caught her hand in mine. "You're right. I've run far and fast and my shadow ran fast, too. Maybe it's time I stopped running."

No one had looked at me the way Pony was looking at me now—not since that bitter day on The Shelf when I stared into the eyes of Warden Duffy.

"I wouldn't know how to start," I said, thinking out loud. "Or how to get my story before people."

"You're to perform at the Shriners' Temple tomorrow night. There's your start," she said.

"But I'm booked as an entertainer," I reminded her. It was my first club date in Kansas City.

"So what? If you have something worthwhile to say, they'll listen. Honey, you profess to believe in a spiritual source of power greater than yourself. Okay, lay it on the line. I'm betting on you, and so is our little girl."

"Anything would be an improvement on the way I feel now," I said. "I'll try it."

"Now, you're putting your money where your mouth is," she said with a quick grin. "If there's one thing I've learned in my job it is how to recognize a story. This, honey, is a story. I'm going down to the newspapers and get them to cover it. You've got something to say that people need to hear, and my job is to convince the city editors of it."

"You sure know how to put on the pressure."

"Bill, the pressure on your back has been building up for the past twenty years. Ever since you came out of San Quentin."

"I guess you're right," I admitted.

"I know I'm right. I know something else which perhaps you've forgotten. Everytime you've been put under real pressure, you've come through—Dallas excepted. But after all, everyone is allowed to lose one fight.

"Remember what Jack Dempsey said, 'Being able to do it isn't enough. You have to be able to do it at nine o'clock on Saturday night in Madison Square Garden.' That's what it is for you tomorrow night—for all of us."

"It isn't tomorrow night any longer," I reminded her. "It's now three o'clock in the morning. That means it's tonight. . . ."

I had never had stage fright in my life. Oh sure, I had had butterflies in my stomach on opening nights. But they were only normal reactions in a strange club, before a strange audience.

As I stood in the wings of the large auditorium, listening to my introduction, I had real stage fright. There was so much at stake. When the master of ceremonies finally introduced me, I offered a silent prayer and walked across the stage to the familiar sound of polite applause from an audience waiting to be entertained.

A thousand shows before a thousand audiences came to my rescue. Automatically, I opened with about three minutes of comedy—the "warm up," it is called. Then, mentally crossing my fingers, I stopped the humor.

"Ladies and gentlemen," I said, "I'm going to make a radical departure from anything I've ever done. Tonight, I want to talk to you in a most serious vein about most important subjects. You, your children and your lives. This will not be rehearsed. Tonight, if you will permit me, I wish to speak with my heart."

I don't know how the words came to me. They came, I am sure, from that Source that is open to everyone who takes a bold step in the direction of right. They were inspired words, words I had never used before. I am able to repeat some of them now, verbatim, because of the newspaper accounts of that evening.

"Tonight, I want to tell you about 'the third step.' The first step society takes with regard to a problem of crime is punishment. The second step comes when society decides punishment is not enough. That conviction has sprung from the hearts and minds of men like Warden Clinton T. Duffy of San Quentin prison, who has reasoned that to punish a man and then turn him loose to harm society again is not the answer. 'Rehabilitate the man,' says Duffy, 'and make him a useful member of society.'

"The third step is, of course, obvious. Prevention. It is on that topic that I am going to speak tonight.

"My right to speak is unique. You see standing before you a man who had the good fortune to be born the only son of a wealthy and politically powerful man. Yet, at the age of 20 I stood with my father by my side before a Superior Court judge and heard myself sentenced to spend the remainder of my life in the California State Penitentiary at San Quentin. Prior to that I had been in reform school. Altogether, I have served nearly four years in jails and prisons.

"I am an ex-convict.

"Almost twenty years ago I was released from San Quentin on parole, and nearly seventeen years ago that parole was discharged. In the intervening years I have led a diamond expedition into Venezuela, coached swimming teams in India, had big business in the United States, entertained in nightclubs, flown airplanes and driven racing cars—and I have contributed nothing.

"Tonight, I would like to change that."

The truths I had learned poured forth in a torrent of words. Some of them were quoted in the papers. Pony told me some; a few I recall myself.

"Some truths are unpleasant to face, like the fact that most parents, even those in this room, are rearing children on a false premise, misleading them, handicapping them to face life as adults.

"This false premise is our system of rewards and punishment for our children. We teach our children—from infancy—to expect to be rewarded for doing what they are supposed to do. For example, we reward a child when he behaves at the dinner table, or when he studies hard, or when he does a hundred other things he is supposed to do. In reality, a child should be punished for doing less than he is supposed to do. For as adults, we are not rewarded for doing what we are supposed to do; we are merely allowed to live. We are punished if we do less. In order to earn rewards, we, as adults, must perform extra service. So what happens to these children who are taught from birth that life rewards them for doing what they are supposed to do? When they grow up, they find that Dear Old Mom and Dad have given them a false foundation upon which to base their lives. What do these kids do when the rose-colored glasses are yanked off?

"They rebel. Or they withdraw, if that is all they can do with the equipment they have been given."

I spoke of facing truths of all kinds. I talked about problem children, recidivism, capital punishment, and I spoke of things spiritual.

"There are certain spiritual laws," the newspapers quoted me as saying, "that are as inexorable as the physical laws of gravity. Your faith or belief or ignorance of them has nothing to do with the fact they are there. Some of these laws may deal with God; others, although they may stem from the same spiritual force, are rules of human behavior that must be learned by every child and every adult who hopes to lead any kind of happy life.

"Every major company in this country has enforced training in the laws of success: positive thinking, getting along with others, good attitudes. Yet not a school, public or private, from first grade through high school, in this entire country offers these teachings to our children. . . ."

I attacked every fiat that has been laid down falsely and, therefore, has contributed to the juvenile problem. To me, these conclusions were obvious.

"Rehabilitation and prevention are one and the same thing. The lessons that must be learned in order to face life happily are the same for the child in school, the young man or woman in college or the convict in a penitentiary. If those lessons are taught in the home, or the church or the school, then we call them prevention. If they are learned in a prison, accompanied by pain and heartbreak, we call them rehabilitation."

I remember speaking of simple ways to teach children.

"Consideration is the key to human happiness. If a child is taught to be truly considerate of others—their feelings, their time, their words, their actions, their rights and their property—what laws or whose commandments can that child break? This lesson should be taught to children as life teaches it to us as adults—with firmness. Expect the child to be considerate. Show him by example."

Early in my speech, when I was talking about my prison background, I had mentioned Caryl Chessman—and my firm belief in his innocence. Now as I spoke of consideration, I saw a way in which Chess, through his death, could contribute something to this audience.

"Let me tell you something about Caryl Chessman, something you have never heard before. I am not going to burden you with a harangue about Chessman's guilt or innocence. That question is now academic, as he is dead.

"There is something, however, that may prove of value to society in the way he died. What I am going to tell you now has never been told in public before.

"Something about the way he died.

"The fact is that after the cyanide pellets were dropped into the vat of acid beneath his chair in the gas chamber, Chessman said one word. A word that was never reported in any newspaper account of his death, including the prize-winning account that was written by my wife.

"That word was never reported simply because it was not possible to do so, clearly, in the space allocated in the terse newspaper accounts of Chessman's death.

"The word was 'No.'

" 'No' what?

" 'No'—don't kill me?

" 'No'—I am innocent?

" 'No'—I don't want to die?

"I will tell you how, in that one word, Caryl Chessman taught **a** lesson from which we can all learn. But let me regress to the last press interview before his date with death, so you can understand this man and that word.

"His last interview was given to my wife. He had invited her to attend the execution. (The condemned man has the curious right to invite five people of his own choosing to attend.)

" 'Why?' my wife asked in that last interview, 'do you want me **to** be there?'

" 'Because it will give you the authority to write about it,' he said. 'No woman has ever witnessed an execution in California. Killing is **a** man's business. The giving of life belongs to women. Perhaps if capital punishment, that evil scar across the face of justice, is ever to be erased, it will be done by women. So I would like you to be there, I would like you to see that it is not a prideful thing . . . if it were, it would be carried out in a public square. I would like you to see the pomp and the punctilio with which a man's life is deliberately snuffed out by the State, in your name, the name of society.'

" 'Chess,' she said, 'if they actually strap you down, close the door and drop the pellets, I don't think I can survive it.' Chess grinned his lopsided smile, and with his wry humor said, 'Neither can I.'

"And so Chess was taken to the 'holding cell,' the night before his death, to await his final date with California's executioner. How did he spend his last night on earth? By ranting and raving against society? By resignedly awaiting his death? He did neither.

"Part of that last night he spent with his attorney, Rosalie Asher, who will tell about their personal conversations in her forthcoming book. Rosalie told me recently, 'He seemed to know that this time it was the end—that it was finally over.'

"When Rosalie had gone, Chess sat down and began to write. It wasn't affidavits he was writing, or legal briefs, or writs or pleas for clemency. These were personal letters he wrote—letters to friends, to be delivered only after his execution.

"He wrote a letter to Rosalie. I have seen it, and she will publish it. It was filled with warmth, kindness and appreciation for all she had done for him. It was a genuine attempt to make her feel better about his passing.

"He wrote a letter to Mary Crawford, a newspaperwoman who

also attended his execution. Published in the San Francisco *News Call Bulletin*, it outlined his last and final thoughts on the problem of juvenile delinquency. It was his last contribution to society. Another note, to reporter Will Stevens, was later published in the *San Francisco Examiner*. It, too, was filled with warmth, empathy, understanding and help for others.

"And still another of those letters was written to my wife. A personal letter not meant for publication. That final request we will not break even now.

"I can, however, tell you that in that letter he said in part: 'I am a singularly fortunate guy to have two such dedicated friends as you and Rosalie.' Soon to die, that man considered himself 'a singularly fortunate guy.'

"Perhaps he was. He, after all, was about to secure his freedom. His unbelievable ordeal of twelve years on Death Row was about to end. I can't help but remember one conversation he had with my wife.

"'. . . I will certainly admit that these twelve long years on Death Row have changed me greatly,' he said. 'They would change anyone. Death Row has given me more than it can ever take away. Many times I have been sorely tempted to quit fighting—to stop trying. It is so simple to die, and so very difficult to live under these circumstances. My pride and the certain knowledge of my innocence have helped me to continue living. It is my pride that rebels at the thought of dying with the smell of peach blossoms—strapped down—gagging —stared at. But I have more than that to keep me going. I have my desire to contribute something really worthwhile through my writing. If this story should turn out to have a grim ending, instead of a happy one, you will see a whole man and not a tortured shell enter that little green room. I'll take much that is good to eternity with me. I also hope I'll leave some that is good behind. I hope that I will still be able to make a worthwhile contribution—even by my death.'

"By maintaining his balance, and even his sense of humor, until the very end, Chess tried to make it a little easier on his friends.

"And so it was that on May 2, 1960, my wife, at Chess' invitation, stood at a window of that little green room, just three feet away from where a man she liked and respected was being strapped to his final chair.

"You have all read the stories of that execution—that his last words were to my wife—of how he tried to make it easier on the warden by saying: 'Thank you, Warden, I am all right.' And how he died, as he said he would, with dignity.

"But what about the 'No'?

"Death in San Quentin's gas chamber is not silent, nor painless nor easy. It took Chessman eight and a half minutes to die and that, by gas chamber standards, was fast. He made it easy on himself as well as others. The pellets were fired audibly into the acid vat and, when that sound was heard, everyone, including the condemned man, knew life had ended for Caryl Chessman.

"It takes time for that gas to be generated and to reach the condemned man's nostrils. Perhaps thirty seconds, perhaps forty-five, but it is an eternity to the man in the chair.

"During that half minute or longer, the man is as fully conscious and as fully aware as you are now. He has not so much as sniffed the invisible fumes. But in moments—and he knows it—he is going to die. He cannot be saved any longer—even by a reprieve. As a matter of fact, the phone rang just thirty seconds after the pellets were dropped, with a reprieve for Chess, but it was too late. Mercifully, he did not know about it.

"So what does a man do with his last half minute of life? Scream? Curse? That would be understandable.

"I will tell you what Chessman did. He turned his head quickly, looked at my wife, who was at the window, and saw her face contort as she was stricken by what was happening to her friend.

"With a great muscular effort he twisted his strapped-down wrists so that with his hands he could give her a 'thumbs up' gesture. Then, with unmistakable intent to help her over this rough spot, he shook his head from side to side and told her 'No-o-o-o.'

"He waited until he saw her face relax. 'If he has the courage to do the dying, I must have the courage to do the watching,' my wife told me she had thought at that awful moment.

"Then, after he saw my wife's face relax, he turned his head as far away from her as he could, so she wouldn't have to see his face, then breathed quickly and deeply. Then quietly and with dignity he got on with the business of dying.

"His final thoughts and words and gestures were for the comfort and peace of mind of someone else.

"Consideration.

"Can we learn anything from that?

"Decide for yourself, each of you."

It was out. That huge auditorium was a vault of silence. Forbidding and absolute.

I had nothing more to say. I knew I had put things bluntly, even shockingly, but also with complete honesty and no compromise of any sort. No defense of my own actions, no accusations against others. How else could I say it? It was my life, as I had lived it. The lessons were what that life had taught me. I had hoped that by overcoming my reserve, by laying my heart and soul bare, I might save someone else that frightful tuition. Well, I had wanted to know whether that life stood for anything or not, and this total silence told me.

I walked off the stage into the wings in complete silence. It was over. I had failed.

Then it came. Like an explosion. Wave after wave of applause. The house lights were turned up. I could see the people in the audience. They were standing. They were cheering. The sound reverberated from wall to wall—the way I had heard it long ago for another man, in a blue suit in a long line of grey.

Pony was in my arms, her wet face pressed to mine. We stood, wordlessly, hanging on to each other in the darkness of the wings. I was weak, exhausted, numb. Only habit ingrained by a thousand night club performances propelled me back onto the stage. There was my audience—still standing and applauding. It went on for what seemed to me like an eternity. The newspaper accounts reported it as a "ten-minute standing ovation." As those people applauded, the innermost part of myself was washed with warmth and humility such as I had never known.

I placed an unsteady hand on the microphone. Once again, silence.

"Ladies and gentlemen . . ." I had to clear my throat. "I wish there were some way for me to express the gratitude that I find in my heart. There is no adequate way. The closest would be to state a simple fact. The fact is that if because of something I said here tonight, just one youngster may be prevented from entering prison instead of college; if just one ex-convict can find the strength to give instead of to take, or if just one child may be kept from some day facing the necessity of having to die—*considerately*—then my time, *all of my time*, has been well spent."

Book
Three

14

DOORS BEGAN TO OPEN. ONE OF THE FIRST
was to a prison.

Not San Quentin this time. Leavenworth Federal Penitentiary. But inside
there were the same grey walls, grey bars,
grey faces. It was after dark as I went
through the main rotunda, accompanied
by two guards. When I heard the heavy
electrically controlled main gates clang
behind me, my palms became clammy.

We went down a concrete and metal
corridor to a small auditorium where from
seventy-five to a hundred cons sat facing
the stage. I was seated in the back.

Free men were on the stage, finishing a

class or program. Then one of them introduced me, and I stepped forward. This time I was wearing a blue suit, white shirt and blue tie. The man described me as "an outsider who has something worthwhile to say."

"Fellows, I was introduced as an outsider," I began. "I don't feel like one. That's because twenty years ago I was Inmate Number 66836 in San Quentin. I was a convicted armed robber, several times over, with a previous record of armed robberies as a juvenile. I served my time then, as you're doing now. And I was also what you call a 'solid con.' I had no use for stool pigeons then, nor do I now. You can guess what my opinion of prison guards was at the time I was beaten by them in San Quentin prison. That basic opinion of brutal guards is unchanged today."

There was a rustle in the room. I saw a few smiles and heard a couple of snickers. I was saying what they wanted to but could not. It gave me their confidence. I glanced at the front row where the associate warden was sitting, but his face was expressionless. I had told him earlier I didn't know what I could accomplish with the men, but, for a certainty, it would accomplish nothing if I couldn't reach them. So I reached them in the only way I knew how. By merging with them. It was no act.

"So you see, I can't talk 'down' to anyone here," I plunged on, "but I would like to make one thing clear. There may be men in this room who are institutionalized—who don't care whether or not they return to prison, if and when they get out. I have nothing to say to them. I am talking to the guys who feel as I felt—who want to get out and stay out. I can tell you how. Would you like to hear?"

The deep-throated "Yes" roared through the room. So I told them —as simply and as honestly as I could. I outlined the studies I had undertaken in San Quentin and the pertinent conclusions I had drawn from them. I told of how that Front Gate had opened. I spoke of truth and consideration. I gave them the highlights of my adventurous life since San Quentin.

"There's all the excitement, adventure and romance you're big enough to handle, and it's all available within the law. My own life proves that. Now, what about you? I know just exactly what every one of you men—without exception—is going to do when you return to your cell. You are going to lie to yourself. You are going to dream wondrous dreams of the outside world. Not a single man among you is going to dream of being on the outside, working for an unfair boss, driving an old car, being in debt and married to someone who doesn't at all resemble a movie queen. It is no fun, I know, to dream about anything other than curvaceous women, fine cars, good jobs and a smooth life.

"But the outside is just the same as it always was. There are still bills to pay and sick kids and old cars that don't work and paychecks that won't quite cover everything. There are still petty people with petty motives who won't forgive you for being an ex-con. All right. Face it. Face life as it really is—not as you wish it were. We can't change the world. We can only change ourselves.

"And another thing. Everything in here is either black or white. Outside it isn't always like that. People you thought might be solid don't always turn out to be. But you can't go and bend a pipe over their heads.

"If you can get to be truly considerate of the other guy's rights, his time, his opinions, his property—how can you go wrong? What law, whose commandment can you break?"

I said that and more. I told them the difference between "smart" and "stupid," "tough" and "mean." It was brutal and it hurt. But it worked. I'd broken through. They took it and they liked it. I was effective because I was one of them, and they knew it. They never would have taken it, no matter how well-intentioned, from the chaplain or the psychiatrist or the warden. But I was an ex-convict.

They tipped over their chairs and rushed forward. Dozens of rough hands reached, simultaneously, to shake mine. Two men whom I had known in San Quentin were present. One had been back to prison three times, the other twice. One grizzled old guy with tears streaking down his face put a hand on my shoulder and patted me, saying over and over: "I just want to touch a guy who was able to stay out."

There was a great press of questions. To try to answer them all was impossible. I stepped back onto the stage and everyone became quiet.

"You know my name. If the day comes, when you're out and you have a problem you can't handle, look me up and we'll kick it around. I don't guarantee I can solve everything. But we'll sure as hell give it a whirl—in complete confidence, of course."

I left the penitentiary feeling warm and good. Afterward I was told I was the only ex-convict ever to address inmates of a Federal prison up to that time. Maybe I had found another way in which I could really help—not just those men, but also the victims that they wouldn't harm if they heeded my words.

The prison talk was the result of my appearance before the Shriners. That evening, a number of listeners had asked me to speak before other groups. I had already made a score of appearances before parent-teacher organizations, service clubs, women's clubs and business luncheon groups. I thought the first flush of enthusiasm following the original talk provided this impetus. But each talk I gave produced a dozen more requests, until I was working far more hours on these dates than on my job.

We had been in Kansas City more than a year since I had given that first talk. I had worked my way from one job to another until I had become the vice-president of a large organization and had put together a national sales program. We now lived in a handsome home in a comfortable suburb, and Bonnie was attending one of the best public schools in the country. It looked as if we were setting down roots.

About two months after my talk at Leavenworth, I had my first ex-convict caller. It was a vicious winter night, and I was glad to get home after giving a lecture on juvenile delinquency. The outside temperature was zero; winds from the Great Plains had torn down branches of our shade trees and piled sparse snow in scallops at our windows and across the wide boulevard. Pony had stayed home because she was unable to get a baby-sitter for Bonnie. I was looking forward to hot coffee and a chance to share with her the evening's experience.

Once inside the door, I realized we had a visitor. Pony was serving coffee to a young man in the living room. As he got up, he unfolded six feet of rawboned, bunch-muscled build. He had sandy hair and a homely, friendly face.

"Hullo, Bill Sands—" he said hesitantly.

"Yes?" I asked.

He introduced himself by a name I will change to Tom and added, "I'm taking you up on the offer you made at Leavenworth. I been tellin' Mrs. Sands I heard about you from a friend . . . that you said if a guy is havin' trouble stayin' out, he could drop by and you'd see if you could help him. That right?"

"That's right." The incredible grapevine inside and outside prison had been functioning. We shook hands. "Sit down. What's your trouble?"

"I'm a 3-time loser. Strong arm robberies. Done more'n eight years altogether in three joints. Been outa 'Q' (the convict's nickname for San Quentin) four months. I come back here where my mother lives. We both thought I could do better here. But today—well, today I got canned from my job when the boss found out I was an ex-con. The son of a bitch, 'scuse me, Mrs. Sands, said he didn't want no ex-cons around and he wouldn't give me my money neither." The friendliness had gone out of his face. It was tight and tough now.

"Go on."

"How's a guy supposed to stay out, if he can't make a living?" His question was explosive.

"Let me ask you a question, Tom. Where would you rather be—locked in a cell in San Quentin or here—broke?"

"Here, of course."

"If you don't like it here, you can walk out the door and go see your mother or your girl friend, if you have one, or just go for a walk. If you have to, you can beg a meal from a café or wash dishes for it. What job did you have in Q?"

"I didn't have any. They kept me in my cell twenty-two hours a day and let me out for two hours in the yard. There was a bunch of us they said wouldn't conform or somethin'. . . ."

"Do you want to go back to Q?"

"Well, I don't want to take a pushin' around just because I'm an ex-con. He thinks I don't dare belt him for canning me and holding my dough 'cause it would get me in trouble. I did a good job for that man. Never showed up late to work or nothin', didn't do no drinkin', polite to everybody. Damn him. I gotta get some money someplace."

"Are you still on parole?"

"No, sir, I ain't on parole. I'm 27 years old and I'm discharged. I did four years on my last rap. I did all my time straight time so I don't owe 'em nothin'."

"Then you can't be violated and sent back just because you're out of a job. Right?"

"You're damn right."

"Are you willing to work?"

"Sure, I'm willin'."

"What can you do?"

"Nothin' special, some of everythin'. Laborer and stuff like that. But I can cook; I been a fry cook."

"If you can get a job and hold it, you can stay out. That's what you want to do?"

"Right."

"All right. I'm going to show you how to tell someone you're an ex-con instead of letting him find it out for himself. A wise man (Big Jim) once told me most people have a blind side. They're like dogs that are friendly unless you come up on that blind side. Then the dog is liable to bite, because he's scared. That's the first thing he does, just by instinct. People are like that, so stay away from their blind side. Let me show you how."

Although it was after midnight, I called two business friends. One of them offered Tom work in a mattress factory. It wasn't much of a job, but it was one he could have as long as he wanted it. There might be a chance for promotion.

"All right, Tom. This guy already knows you're an ex-con and he's willing to give you a chance. There are lots of people like that; they'll give you a chance, if you'll just give them a chance. If you had gone to work for this same man, and he had found out later you're an ex-con, he'd probably have been angry and fired you. Not for being an ex-con, but for lying to him. Now you have a job you can keep—if you'll work at it."

Tom thanked me, but he made no motion to leave.

"Something else on your mind?"

"I heard you were solid, that you wouldn't say nothin' if I told you somethin'. Well, you know how it is. Who the hell can you talk to that'll understand 'ceptin' someone who's done time? I been hanging around with some guys. . . ." Tom shot a sidelong look at Pony, who suddenly decided she had something to do elsewhere in the house. After she left, Tom lowered his voice and said: "A coupla friends a mine got a job—a big place—all picked out. Can't tell you much about it 'cause I don't know it all myself. But it's a real big haul. Enough for me to get outa the country and quit."

"Tom, I don't need to know anything about it in order to tell you this. I don't say that no one in the world is smart enough to pull one perfect job and quit. I'll just say you're not that smart."

He wasn't and he knew it.

"So when you go that route, Tom, you pull a job and live it up for a little while with the money you get. By the time the heat dies down you're broke again. Then you have to pull another job because that's the way you get your living. It isn't going to be any different than before. You'll pull a few—perhaps get away with them. Then you'll fall on one.

"You know, Tom, as well as I do, that if you make one mistake you're cooked. Yet cops can make a thousand mistakes and if they're right just one time, you're still cooked. The odds are all cockeyed against you. I know you have more brains than that, or you wouldn't be here talking to me. When you start pulling jobs, you're starting on the way back."

"Yeah, I know."

As we talked, I shot at him with a verbal scatter gun, using every argument I knew on the folly of taking that route at all. It was after 3 in the morning when he finally indicated he was ready to leave.

I offered to drive him home.

"Thanks anyway," he declined. "I feel better. Maybe I can make it. You're the only one who ever talked to me like this. Everyone else always yaps about what's right. But by God, I can see now where maybe it's just plain dumb."

We shook hands, and he left. I was lost in deep thought, staring out of the front picture window, when Pony came in.

"Honey, I heard part of what was said, and I'd like to know why you never pointed out right versus wrong. Don't you think he's bright enough to grasp that?" she asked.

"He knows what it means, all right. But he's not ready to hear it yet. All he's thinking about is what's smart and what's dumb. He has a certain amount of pride and ego—at times that's about all men in prison have, so he has to have 'smart' to hang onto. 'Good' won't do it right now. If he can stay on the right track long enough, the time will come when he'll correlate 'right' to 'smart' and 'wrong' to 'dumb.' *The world insists on his being something that, so far, it hasn't permitted him to be.* His pride and stubbornness, together with his real desire to stay out, are all I have to work with. What he has, can become determination if handled correctly. Otherwise, it is blind bullheadedness. For instance, can you think of anyone of our acquaintance who would turn down a ride home on a night like this? Of course, not. But he has to have something of his own, something to take pride in. His values are mixed up, and the treatment he's been getting hasn't helped. Maybe I can do him some good."

"I don't know about Tom, but I know you're doing someone some good. Think about the people who won't get hit over the head and robbed tonight. That's something."

"That's my girl," I said with a grin. "Incidentally, honey, how come you let him in before I came home? He's such a big, rough-looking customer, I wouldn't have blamed you if . . ."

She interrupted me with her happy, Pony-type logic: "You never have to worry about me or my judgment. Before I let him in, I made sure he was an ex-convict!"

Four days later, Tom was back, grim-faced and tough. He had a newspaper and as soon as we were alone he slapped it down on the coffee table in front of me.

"Look at that. Right there on the front page. Two hundred thousand, they got. Four guys—that's fifty grand apiece. That's what you talked me out of."

There it was, apparently a perfectly planned and executed robbery. The newspaper was painstakingly thorough. Four armed, masked men had been in the payroll office for less than thirty seconds. Each man had an assigned post and task. In half a minute they were gone with nearly a quarter of a million dollars. Police found the getaway car a mile from the scene and surmised a second getaway car also had been used. There were no fingerprints, no useable descriptions—practically nothing for police to go on. It looked as if this job certainly would have solved Tom's immediate problem.

"Four guys, just four guys," Tom was repeating ruefully. He looked at me accusingly.

"Pretty damn slick." I appeared to agree. Tom and I believed it had been an inside job. Probably a former employee, familiar with the office, had been the finger man. He would not have been one of the four because he would be recognized.

"That makes five guys, altogether," I surmised. Tom didn't argue the point. I mused aloud, "Now, I'm wondering about the getaway car. You don't suppose they left it, a hot car without a driver, trusting to luck to get the keys out and get it started? And they sure as hell wouldn't have left it with the motor running and call attention to it, would they?"

"Man, no. They'd have a driver, sure."

"That makes six guys," I noted.

Then we started wondering about the second getaway car the paper had mentioned. It must have had a driver, also.

We recapitulated. Four stickup men, one finger man, two drivers. That made seven. . . .

"Hey, we forgot the lookout. They'd have had one in any job like this." Tom thought of it. That made eight men. The two hundred thousand now would be split eight ways instead of four.

"Twenty-five grand ain't to be sneezed at, though." Tom was still disappointed he was not a partner.

"I'll say it isn't." I was honest with him. "I just thought of something else. How about a big payroll like that? You can bet some of it came directly from the bank, with serial numbers recorded."

"You can always fence it." Tom had been around the block before.

"What's the price now, cool money for hot?" I asked.

"About half," he said knowledgeably. He beat me to the next, obvious conclusion. "Eight guys dividing a hundred comes to twelve five apiece. But that's still better than nothin'."

"It sure as hell is. You can't find anyone who will argue with that, Tom. There'd be only a couple of worries I'd have if I'd been in on it. . . ." I let my voice trail off.

"For one thing, $12,500 isn't enough to get you out of the country and keep you anyplace long. There'd be the matter of a passport. Anyone fresh out of a joint couldn't get one; too many agents watching. Hey, Tom, I forgot to ask you—don't you still attract official attention whenever anything happens in this vicinity?"

"Oh, sure. Them cops picked me up four times for showups. But I never been pointed out—course, I ain't done nothin', but that don't keep them square johns from sayin' it was you—even if you don't look like the guy who did it."

I knew.

I went on, "With the cops watching you so closely, even if no one identified you in a showup what would you do with the money? If you bought a new car, they'd be on you like tigers. Same with a lot of new clothes or a new house for your mother. They'd know you couldn't have saved that much by checking what you had been paid on your various jobs. So what would you do with it?"

"I could put it in a can in my backyard and take out just enough to live on every week for quite a while before I'd have to go ask some dummy for a job again." Tom was tenacious, but not dishonest with me or himself.

"Okay," I said. "It isn't very glamorous, like flying to Rio de Janeiro and living it up. But you wouldn't have to work for a while if you lived on your present standard, although you can do better than that with a steady job. But you know what I'd be worrying about?"

"What now?" he asked wearily.

"I'd be wondering about those seven other guys. I'd wonder if any one of them would do something stupid and get picked up for it. Could you bet your life, that is the remainder of your life on the outside, that he wouldn't sing? Do you know them all that well? Hell, the reward on recovering $200,000 might tempt him. If the guy turned state's evidence and gave back his dough and helped recover all the rest by ratting on the others, he'd stand to come off pretty good. . . ."

Tom threw up his hands and admitted I was correct. He wanted basically to stay on the right track. His coming to me proved it. He just needed a little help to keep him there. The payoff came three days later when the robbery was solved and the men were arrested. Eight of them. One man, an unrealistic candidate for the role of a millionaire, had been throwing around one-hundred-dollar bills. He was questioned—and sang, implicating all the others. Tom telephoned me to be sure I had seen the story. He was happy. And he was free.

"A happy ending!" Pony declared delightedly, executing a cartwheel in the living room.

But her high spirits took a sudden dive two nights later while we were entertaining a school principal and his wife. The former had invited me to speak at a convention of school teachers. When the telephone rang, Pony answered it in the hallway. She formed the word "Tom" with her lips and walked off beyond our earshot with the telephone.

But she was back in the living room in seconds. With one rigid arm she held the instrument out to me, her hand still over the mouthpiece, and then lay flat on her back on the floor in a gesture of total defeat and announced: "It's Tom. He says 'I gotta racket, been workin' it for two days and your old man can't shoot no holes in this one. I'll prove it to him. I tell yuh I'm workin' it—lemme talk to him.'"

"Yes, Tom." I waited, fingers crossed.

"Hey, man, you know where all these rich square johns live out in Leawood and Prairie Village?" He was referring to two of the most exclusive residential areas near Kansas City.

"Yes," I answered in a low voice.

"Well, you know how they live in those hundred grand houses and all." I knew.

"Got me a racket with 'em," Tom went on. "Boy am I laughin' at these suckers."

"What kind of racket, Tom?"

"I gotta tell you about this. I'm makin' twice as much loot in my spare time as I am at the mattress factory. You can't shoot no holes in this."

"Go on, Tom."

"Well, I get out to Leawood, see, and I go up and ring a doorbell. If the maid answers the door, I tell her 'I wanna see the lady o' the house.' When the lady comes—man, you'll die. . . ."

"I'm dying already. What do you do next?"

"I tell her, 'Lady,' I say, 'your driveway and walk is all slippery with snow. Somebody's liable to break their neck out there. Whaddya say I clean it off? I'll do both the driveway and the walk for five bucks.'

"And, Bill, these dumb square johns don't think nothin' of givin' me a fin for it. Hell, I can do one whole place in thirty minutes. Made forty bucks yesterday and thirty-five so far today. How's that for a racket? Geez, if this snow just keeps up, I'm rich."

"That's great, Tom. I have an idea. D'you suppose those squares would pay you this summer for doing their lawns? If they'll shell out five bucks for thirty minutes, they ought to pay you more for an hour or so work—probably let you do it with their mowers, too."

"Hey, that's great. I bet they would. But right now, pray for it to keep snowin', willya?"

"I'll sure do that, Tom," I promised. And I meant it.

It took Pony and me several minutes to put our guests together again. They had been almost demoralized by Pony's antics and our conversation. After they left Pony turned on the outdoor floodlights and gazed at the swirling white that presaged a blizzard. I stood behind her, my arms around her, and watched the Christmas card scene.

"Isn't that snowfall beautiful?" she said dreamily.

"Honey, that's the greatest understatement since Noah said, 'It looks like rain.'"

15

TOM WAS ONLY THE FIRST OF MANY. THERE were talks in other prisons, and requests for me to address groups continued to pour in. For every appearance, from two to ten parents of problem youngsters found their way to me. Ex-convicts were sent by Dale Carnegie and the Alcoholics Anonymous groups who worked in prisons. Ex-convicts were sent by each other. Or they came on their own.

We had a 16-year-old boy living with us for three weeks, an alcoholic school teacher for two and an unemployed cowboy, who had just been released and whose 5-day stay was marred by the fact that his happy round face was due to a case of mumps.

Then I had a failure.

Ricky was 16, tall, well built, of good family. He had been a leader, both scholastically and athletically—not only in his high school but in statewide competition. I worked with him for a month. After that he slipped from sight, so I'll address this to him personally, in the hope he will read it and, perhaps, give me some answers.

Ricky, where did I fail you? We both thought you "had it made," remember? When I asked what thrill there was to be found in stealing hubcaps and credit cards, what you expected in the way of resistance from an unoccupied automobile, you ultimately decided that your only "thrill" was in doing something wrong.

Remember the day I borrowed the Ferrari race car and taught you how to corner and let you drive at 155 miles an hour on the drag strip? Remember the little 2-place airplane I rented and how we hedgehopped and took a run at the row of trees, pulling up just in time? Those were some of the things I had found thrilling—legitimate, legal ways for a young man to let off steam. You agreed, too, and obtained your Dad's permission to take flying lessons. Remember?

But what happened, Ricky? I didn't hear from you for about a month. Then, just two weeks ago, when I was at the jail to visit another boy about your age, the big jailer there, the one who liked you so much, told me you were somewhere in Texas, convicted of stealing an automobile—a felony.

My failure with you, Ricky, brought home to me an understanding of Warden Duffy that I had never had before. It made me realize that one victory in the battle for men's minds is worth a hundred defeats. It has brought me closer to Warden Duffy than I have ever been.

But, Ricky, how about you? Where do we go from here? How many years, how many broken hearts, how much pain will you cause and will you suffer? Will you have to go to the very end, the way Chessman did, to learn the rules that must be followed in order to have a happy life?

Once, when Pony said to him, "I don't know why you have to

die," Chess answered, "Pony, if I do, it is because I've found myself too late."

Ricky, how many young men like you have to die in order to learn how to live?

My days and nights were filled with talks, all of them rushing me toward an inevitable decision. It was a radio program that finally caused me definitely to make up my mind.

Jean Glenn, the sparkling mistress of ceremonies of Station WDAF in Kansas City, had me in her guest spot for an hour on a program called "Conversation." Three weeks later we did a 2-hour "live" program in which open telephone lines permitted listeners to call and ask questions while we were on the air. Calls lit up the station switchboard like a Times Square marquee. Mail arrived by the bagful. Jean introduced me as the vice-president in charge of sales and named my company, producing total havoc on our business switchboard and causing the mail clerk to threaten to enlist in the Army.

I was convinced I really did have something to say and, because I am by nature impatient, I began to wax wroth when it became apparent that I could not reach every parent in the country in one day. After Pony had heard my restless muttering for the thousandth time, she suggested in her typically direct way:

"Go write a book."

To fit the writing of a book into a schedule that already was bursting at the seams was patently impossible. Something had to give, and it looked as if it would be me. Pony agreed:

"If you keel over dead you won't be of any help to anyone. And besides, I'd be mad at you."

I needed to talk to Warden Duffy. And I determined to make the time to do it. I cut all ties for two weeks and telephoned him that I was coming to California and bringing Pony and Bonnie with me. It had been more than a dozen years since I had seen the Duffys. Deep within me I knew why. In my subconscious I had always envisioned myself riding back on a white charger and laying something grand at their feet. But now in my struggle, not for the personal success I had always wanted to show them, but for something far more important—the chance to make a real contribution—I headed for that rock of integrity where I could seek, and get, advice and reassurance.

We made a date to meet in San Francisco's St. Francis Hotel. The plush lobby and its busy, well-dressed people dropped away when I saw the Warden and his wife approaching. They were just the same, except that his iron-grey hair was now a cap of white. For an odd moment as they came toward us I felt like applauding as I used to. Then they were there. He gave me his warm, firm handshake and Mom was looking at me the way she had that evening in another lifetime.

"This is just like coming home again," Pony exclaimed as she kissed them both.

At dinner I told them of my dilemma.

"I cannot give up this program of talks, but I feel my first duty is to Pony and Bonnie. It just doesn't make sense for me to resign a good job, gamble on income derived from speeches and plunge into this full time. And now we think I should write a book. I have to give up either my life or my livelihood. . . ."

"Bill," the Warden was looking at me as he had in my solitary cell. "When I first met you, you thought you were at the absolute bottom. I told you then, and I tell you now—when we are thinking right, trying to contribute, doors *do* open. The Front Gate did. Remember?"

"If I can just take care of my family . . . they aren't after me for luxuries, you know. I would only like to give them a small degree of security and at the same time do something that offers a real contribution. Then I would be happy. Truly happy."

"You will do both, make your contribution and support your family. I know you will," the Warden was saying. "Go ahead and write your book. Make your talks. Make whatever arrangements are necessary to give you the time you need. It will come right." His warm voice gave me the same transfusion of life and hope it always had. And Mom Duffy reached across the table and squeezed my hand.

After dinner, when we were in their home and I had been outlining the mechanics of what would be necessary in order for me to launch a new career, Bonnie, who had been listening intently to everything, piped up.

"Daddy, may I say something?" She was careful about interruptions. "You said we would probably have to sell our house and our other car and that you would be gambling everything you had to make this a success. Right?"

"Yes, honey."

"Well, wouldn't it be a contribution, wouldn't it help with money, if we sold my horse?"

She was referring to her beloved "Banner," the spirited palomino quarter horse we had bought her after she proved she was a natural equestrienne. She was one of the few who could really master the big gelding. And she loved that horse, as a child, once in a lifetime, loves an animal. She had entered him in barrel-racing and pole-bending competition, and she adored grooming him and showing him off in the black-and-silver parade saddle and fancy tack we had given her. This was what she now offered.

"If you need any more expression of faith than that, you are not as bright as I think you are." Mrs. Duffy had crossed the room and put her arms around the little girl.

In high spirits we drove to Kansas City and made arrangements for our new life, which included the writing of this book. I gave up my job and we put most of our possessions up for sale, including Banner because Bonnie reminded her mother: "You said when we married Daddy that I get one half of the marriage."

And more doors opened. Within three days of our return, two spokesmen from different school districts in one county where I had addressed P.T.A. meetings came to discuss the possibility of inaugurating success courses at high school and junior high school levels. Discussions with school board officials followed, and I was informed that the classes were to get under way within a year. A juvenile court judge invited me to sit on the bench with him and hear some cases.

Jim Emerson, editor of a community newspaper, asked me to write two series of articles—one on capital punishment, the other on juvenile delinquency. It was at this point Pony and I found we could work together, successfully. We knew that many couples, no matter how close in their marriage, cannot work well together on a project outside their home life. But we found that we could. What had looked like an immense and unfamiliar task, writing the newspaper articles, was duck soup for Pony, but she insisted that I do most of the writing, only giving me pointers and reasons for her editing as we went along.

We were tremendously encouraged, but work on the book had come to a standstill. The demands on our time in Kansas City were such that often we couldn't even get together until late at night, let alone write a book.

We made another decision, a costly one in terms of money. But in answer to Pony's "is this going to be an all-out effort or isn't it?" we packed our things and departed for a remote area in Nevada, where we were not known, in order to do our writing. We installed ourselves in a small motel less than a mile from a stable where Bonnie could ride, then went to work.

Looking backward, I began to see my life in its proper perspective. An interesting thing I had told no one was that I realized early that I had come to evaluate men in a way that would horrify some and amuse others. Lacking Big Jim's psychic faculty, I had to have some means of figuring out what kind of men I was dealing with, how they would react under given sets of circumstances, their solidity and so forth.

The only accurate barometer I had been able to devise was to figure mentally "What kind of a convict would he be?" Then, in my mind, I would strip him of his surroundings, his office, home, car, family, friends, even his clothes. Behind him would rise the cold steel and concrete of San Quentin's Main Yard. My subject would be standing there in a prison uniform. Picturing him thus, I would know what sort of man he was—bully, chicken, stoolie or solid.

At such moments the old animal wariness that had kept me alive would zero him in. I had to be right the first time in my dealings with people. True, I had buried the animal instincts that once had been my means of survival, but they were buried alive. By concentration I could call on them. And I still do.

This barometer has proved invaluable over the years.

During our work I relived the incidents of my childhood, the years of total confinement, the escapades since prison and my recent days of decision.

We returned to Kansas City after seven weeks in which we accomplished the major work on the book. All that remained were minor revisions and some typing—plus what I am writing now.

Before we had gone to Nevada, all our efforts had been unofficial. Now, abruptly, this changed. Jim Emerson, the editor who had become a close friend, took me to the Kansas State Penitentiary to meet the Protestant chaplain, the Reverend James E. E. Post. Jim, as the chaplain insisted I call him, is neither the usual minister nor the usual man. He is big; he is rugged and unshockable. There is warm rapport between him and the men behind the walls.

"I've heard you on the radio," he said. "I believe you have an inspired message. What can I do to help you?"

I told him my ideas about rehabilitation and prevention being one and the same, and I described my visit to the Federal prison.

"I would like to see a class started for men who are about to be released, a class in which they can begin to learn some of the lessons they must know in order to get along on the outside. Every man who comes out must face certain truths. Such as the fact that society insists that a convict be something that society, itself, is reluctant to permit him to be. Fair or unfair, reasonable or unreasonable, there it is. It is tough enough to get around or cope with when you know about it—it is hopeless if you don't.

"He has to learn that he is going back to the same world he left, the same world he could not adjust to before. The world has not changed in his absence; if he is to merge with it, *it is he who has to do the changing.*

"Such classes should be conducted by ex-convicts rather than correctional authorities. For two good reasons. One, because such a man knows what must be done, knows what it feels like to be out in the world, branded with a felony record; and two, because the men inside prisons refuse, for the most part, to take moral lessons from the so-called do-gooders.

"Alcoholics Anonymous has solved this problem for many drinkers, utilizing the principle of one man helping another who shares the same problem. And *all* men released from prison face some of the same problems, whether or not they drink."

"Suppose we get permission to try here?" the chaplain asked.

"Then I'll conduct the first class and turn it over as quickly as possible to other men who have made it on the outside. Eventually men who have attended the class will come back to prison and help conduct it."

"Why can't you stay and run it yourself?" he wanted to know.

"Jim, deep in my heart I know that every time I address a college or a high school or a group of teachers and parents I am doing more good by prevention than I would if I tied myself down to one class in one prison. I think I can do both for a while. I can spend the first three to six months here, but after that I want to go on to other prisons and, at the same time, continue to talk to colleges, high schools and parents."

That was the start, there in the chaplain's office. The following day he made an appointment for us in Topeka with Robert J. Kaiser, director of Kansas penal institutions. After a 4-hour interview the latter gave us the green light to start a class in the State Penitentiary.

A variety show was my means of announcing formation of a pre-release class in the 100-year-old fortress-like structure at Lansing. I called on old friends in show business to donate their time, and Jim Emerson garnered statewide coverage by the major news media. The show was the only way I could think of to get the entire prison population to hear my announcement about the proposed class.

Changing from the fast, bright tempo of a variety show to the serious announcement involved some ticklish moments. I didn't want the men to feel the entertainment had been used to pull them in to hear a preachment. Of course I intended no preachment, but the proposed class depended to a great extent on how these men, many understandably distrustful, would interpret what I said. You could have heard the proverbial pin drop during the first few moments when I identified myself.

I laid it on the line, telling them about my days in reform school, the beating by prison guards that hadn't turned me into a stool pigeon, solitary confinement, consecutive sentences, Warden Duffy.

Three men there had been in San Quentin when I was and knew what I said was true. One, whom I'll call Mac, had worked in the same office with Chess and me—he later turned out to be an invaluable assistant in the class.

I told them about the work I had done on myself, and how it led to serving three life sentences within three years; and I told them about after prison, the fantastic life of adventure and my happy marriage. Then I said I had been given permission to start the proposed class there and, after advising the television and newspaper photographers to train their cameras on the audience, this is what I said to the men who filled the big hall.

"Every wise guy I know is in prison. There are a lot of pretty smart cons in here, penitentiary big shots, who can give you advice. They can tell you how you could have beat your rap if you'd been smarter. They know all about how to outwit the law. They sneer at guys like me, call us square johns, dummies.

"Okay, I'll settle for being a square john, a dummy. But when I leave here this afternoon I'm going to drive off in my air-conditioned car and I'll play a round of golf before dark. Then I'm going to my home. It's air-conditioned too. (These were white lies, as I had sold both the car and the home in order to afford to be there.)

"At home I'll be greeted by my lovely red-haired wife and my cute, little blonde daughter. Before I go to bed I'll have a steak dinner, probably call a couple of friends on the telephone, watch television for a while and have a highball or two if I feel like it.

"I've been a con, as smart and as tough as they come. And I'm still solid. But I'm not a wise guy anymore. I'm a square john now. All the wise guys I know are in here—the smartest ones of all didn't even come to the show, they're in the hole—all the wise guys will go back to their cells and all us dumb square johns will have to leave and go away in our big cars to our nice homes and good pay and lovely wives. Yeah. All us square johns are on the outside."

It was brutal and it hurt. But it worked. I had broken through. Then I put them to the final test.

"In this pre-release class you can learn how to be law-abiding square johns—dummies, like me—willing to earn an honest living and become a useful member of society. How many guys want that?"

The throaty roar was instantaneous and overwhelming. Every man was on his feet, jumping, cheering, applauding. And the cameras recorded it all. So much for those who, *without ever having seen their first convict*, argue that men in prison don't want to change, have no desire to be honest.

The class was a bonus and I was grateful I had the time to get it started. And grateful is a weak word for my feelings toward Jim

Post, Robert Kaiser and Warden Sherman H. Crouse. Thanks to their courage, Kansas took a giant step forward in the history of penology in this country. It wasn't easy. The ensuing weeks took a lot out of all of us. The news media, by and large, were fair. Some were enthusiastic, and some even took editorial stands in favor of the new program.

We squelched a voice or two—the inevitable accompaniment to any penological forward step—that started to cry "criminal coddling"; we pointed out that if anyone were being coddled it was society—that the men were giving of their free time to attend the class.

Eligible men were those due to be released by discharge or parole within ninety days. About 90 percent of the eligibles, some ninety-three men, were in attendance at the first class. We held a 2-hour session every week. At first quite a number of them were suspicious, wondering what my "angle" might be. A few tried me on for size to see if I could be persuaded to bring in contraband or smuggle out letters. Others asked me outright what I was "getting" out of it. Bitterness too long pent up showed itself in that they could not believe anyone would do something for a bunch of convicts unless there were some income to be gained, above or below the table. Be it to their everlasting credit, these men, most of whom experience had taught to be distrustful, took me at my face value.

Each Monday I drove out to the prison early enough to give private counseling to men with special problems. At 6 P.M. we would start our 2-hour sessions. A few penitentiary big shots who came to jeer were drowned out by the men who were eager for the truth. At first resentments accumulated through the years exploded, but before long the first group settled into a unit and hammered out a 7-step program of their own, which was to guide them in maintaining their freedom. These men ranged from first-timers in prison, who had been there only a couple of years, to 5-time losers, some of whom had served more than twenty-five years—from petty theft offenders to men who were criminals before I was born. It was a good cross section and a good group to forge the creed by which they, and those who followed them, could live. It was agreed that each word of each step had to be approved unanimously before it was adopted. Here they are:

1. *Facing* the truth about ourselves and the world around us, we decided we needed to change.

2. *Realizing* that there is a Power from which we can gain strength, we have decided to use that Power.

3. *Evaluating* ourselves by taking an honest self-appraisal, we examined both our strengths and our weaknesses.

4. *Endeavoring* to help ourselves overcome our weaknesses, we enlisted the aid of that Power.

5. *Deciding* that our *freedom* is worth more than our resentments, we are using that Power to help free us from those resentments.

6. *Observing* that daily progress is necessary, we set an attainable goal toward which we could work each day.

7. *Maintaining* our own *freedom*, we pledge ourselves to help others as we have been helped.

The first letters of the steps combine to spell *FREEDOM*.

On cards the men carry—that I carry, too—are the legends "If the 'outside' world only matched our 'inside' dreams, then not one of us would ever return to prison," and "Happiness is a direction—not a place."

On the reverse side of the card is the reminder: "Think realistically."

The class motto was supplied by Jim Post. It is paraphrased from the Bible: "Know the truth and the truth shall make you free."

My guys know it isn't the truth that makes you free—it's the *knowledge* of it.

(To delineate what goes into inspiring or inducing a desire to rehabilitate and then encouraging and nurturing that desire would take a book in itself. And because this involves the same lessons that would have prevented the crimes in the first place, it is a book, for the consumption of teen-agers and their parents. I have already been drafted to write such a book.)

We were able to start a sponsorship program. Under existing laws men have to have jobs before being released on parole. And frequently men were still in prison futilely trying to get jobs—months and even years after the parole board had pronounced them fit to be free. The longest wait for any I knew personally was thirty-four months—he had spent more time trying to get a job after he had been paroled than some men spend in prison altogether. And many men I knew had waited as long as a year to eighteen months.

Under the sponsorship program, I interested some Kansas City businessmen in taking men out and financing them until they could get jobs. Terms of this sponsorship required that the man repay his businessman-sponsor before the latter could take another man. The laws remain the same, but we obtained official permission for this program, thus freeing parolees to compete for jobs by presenting themselves for interviews instead of sending applications from prison. With maintenance of a man in prison costing more than $1,500 a year, the dollar savings were noted almost immediately.

Six months after the program started, only one man, who had a serious drinking problem, had failed to repay his sponsor, and none of the approximately one hundred men who had gone through the class had returned to prison. That is the score at the time this book goes to press.

The prison sessions had taken a great deal of time from speaking engagements, but the bonuses of inner gratification can never be measured in either time or money. (There was none of the latter.) After almost six months I was able to turn the class over to the competent hands of two other men who had served time in that very prison (one of them a 3-time loser), but who had made their own turnabouts and were successful businessmen after almost ten years of freedom. Incidentally, both these men are members of Alcoholics Anonymous, therefore their anonymity is being preserved.

The night I said farewell to the class we singled out Jim Emerson, who had attended all sessions faithfully and who had procured jobs for a large percentage before the sponsorship program was under way, and conferred upon him the degree of "honorary convict." It was hard to tell who was more pleased, the heterogeneous students or the modest newspaperman.

As I said, the prison class was a bonus; now I am back doing what I am best suited for. Speaking to people who are parents and who are going to be parents, and to civic groups and universities already dedicated to education and the betterment of society—truly concerned, thinking, receptive people who act on the lessons my life is able to impart.

A rewarding day at the college level occurred recently at the State College of Iowa in Cedar Falls. I met my host, the dean of the college, at 8:30 A.M., and we were together until almost midnight. My day included two addresses to the student body, three sociology and criminology classes, an after-dinner talk, a radio broadcast that resulted in many requests for a rebroadcast, which in turn brought on an impromptu social gathering and late-evening informal address in the home of a local judge of the criminal court.

In the classes came the penetrating questions. I have learned to expect them, and I'll guarantee that today's college students give the lie to the statement that America's youth concerns itself solely with glittering superficialities. Again and again the stimulating questions and attitudes of these young men and women reflect the tremendous potential of a still-young country. The following are typical of the question and answer sessions:

Q.: "What would you do if you were in charge of sentencing and prisons in the United States today?"
A.: "I would probably be a very unpopular man with a certain segment of the prison population, because I would make every sentence indeterminate, going from one year to life.

"A man may have committed a very serious crime, but if in one year he has rehabilitated himself so that he will never commit that or any other crime again, why hold him any longer? On the other hand, a man's offense may be comparatively minor, but if he will only do the same thing over and over again when freed, why release him?"

Q.: "Isn't that the purpose of parole boards, to release men before they serve their maximum time, if they can be deemed trustworthy?"
A.: "That is one of the reasons behind the formation of parole boards."

Q.: "They don't seem to be working so well; at least many men released this way commit crimes again. How would you rectify that?"
A.: "I would install, in the places of men now on parole boards, M. D. psychiatrists, polygraph (lie detector) operators and men skilled in the use of sodium pentothal, hypnotism and every other technological advance that probes the human mind. Since a convicted felon

has been stripped of his citizenship and therefore of most of his rights, he would be required to undergo tests that could determine his state of mind and whether or not he would be likely to return to crime.

"If he refused to take the tests he would not be considered for parole. If he took them and failed to pass, he would be shown why, with a tape recording of his interview while under sodium pentothal.

"To go hand in hand with this I would initiate prison courses. Their subject matter would be similar to, but not limited to, that covered in the course I installed in the Kansas State Penitentiary, with one very important addition: These sessions would be available to men upon their entry into prison and throughout their stay there, not merely a matter of weeks before their release."

Q.: "How do present parole boards go about finding out if the men will return to crime again?"
A.: "They ask them."

Q.: "You mean parole board members sit there and ask, 'Have you learned your lesson?' 'Do you think you will ever return to criminal ways?' "
A.: "That's exactly what I mean. It is not always that obvious, but any man going before a parole board knows what the board wishes to find out. In fact, any man in any prison in the country knows how to get out in the shortest possible time. He keeps his nose clean, behaves within the rules (or at least doesn't get caught if he violates them), participates in sports or something that will reflect well on his record and reasons out the best way he can express himself in telling the parole board that prison was a good thing for him, that it stopped him just in time, that he is full of remorse and contrition and will never again return to crime.

"Danger also lies in parole board members becoming case-hardened and treating all men as con artists who are trying to outsmart them. Some of the men who come before them are sincere. Only an expert, asking much more subtle questions, can distinguish between the two. Thoughts and attitudes need to be tested as to whether a man tends toward violent solutions of his problems, whether he would be inclined to excesses or abnormality in seeking sexual gratification and so forth. Many men in prison, although not psychotic, are mentally or emotionally disturbed and need psychiatric help. Under this plan they would get it."

Q.: "What is the national rate of recidivism in this country?"

A.: "Statistics tell us that more than 80 percent of the men now in prison for the first time will return to prison after they have been released. As a matter of fact, 87 percent of the men in the Kansas State Prison at Lansing have been in prison before. This is almost total failure.

"Ninety-seven percent of all men in prisons are going to be released sometime. That means they are going to be your neighbors. Punishment and vengeance alone do not make them good neighbors. So let's use our existing facilities and existing knowledge to truly rehabilitate. That is one certain way to lower our crime bill."

Q.: "How do you teach a child with a happy and carefree childhood to think realistically?"

A.: "I can answer that question with a question: How do you learn to get along in the world if knowledge of the world is kept from you? To be more specific, Philip Wylie, in his book *Generation of Vipers*, tells us that slaphappiness is not happiness. And, in my opinion, no truer words were ever spoken. Read his book. It may shock you in some areas, but it is damned hard to argue against, successfully."

Q.: "Do you advocate telling children about the evils of the world, such as the hydrogen bomb and the possible annihilation of the human race, the threat of Communism and things like that?"

A.: "At an age when they can grasp what it is about, I feel they should be informed, yes. You understand these things, yet have you given up working for a degree, your interest in the opposite sex and all plans for marriage and a career in order to dwell on them full time?

"A more immediate threat to children is the possibility of being hit by an automobile. Far more people have been killed by cars than by nuclear warfare. But you don't let your child go heedlessly into the street because you think you will be breaking bad news to him if you warn him about automobiles. You don't believe it is best to keep him in ignorance, blissful ignorance, of traffic until the day he is killed or maimed, do you?

"Of course not. You do everything you can to prepare him because you know you can't always be there to protect him. The same answer, exactly, applies to Communism. The child has to understand something about it in order to realize it is a threat to a better way of life.

"One of the classic lines of all time, in my opinion, was given by an old friend of mine, a man I first knew as 'Hardway.' He said:

" 'Communism would be fine—if God ran it.' "

Q.: "Explain why you are against capital punishment."
A.: "Briefly: It is wrong. Two wrongs do not make a right. It does not deter; it does just the opposite in many, many instances, acting as an incentive instead of a deterrent. For instance, if a man compels someone to move during a robbery, even from just one room to another, it can be called kidnapping. Kidnapping is sometimes punishable by death. So if a criminal thinks his crime may be interpreted as a capital offense, he reasons he has nothing more to lose if he kills the witness, thereby reducing his chances of getting caught. And men who have already killed do not hesitate to do so again, reasoning 'They can only burn me once.'

"To some young hoodlums it is a death-defying and glamorous challenge. Spending years in prison is not so glamorous, they feel. Ask any man who has been in prison whether he would prefer the death penalty or life behind bars and he will, invariably, say 'Give me death.'

"You should ask my little girl. When she was four years old and her mother was covering the Chessman case, one day she asked, 'Mommy, can a good man be bad sometimes?' When she received an affirmative reply, she went on, 'Then can't a bad man be good sometimes, too?' Again after an affirmative, she said, 'Then if we kill him, how can he be good again?'

"Everyone agrees we should know more about the criminal. We cannot find out more by killing him. The trouble with the death penalty, moral issues aside, is that we cannot get rid of the problem by getting rid of the man.

"Ladies and gentlemen, the reasons for abolishing capital punishment would fill a book. In fact they have filled several. I suggest you read them."

Q.: "Is there anything encouraging to tell children about life?"
A.: "Certainly. That's what I dwell on when I address parents. Whether existing facts are encouraging depends more on attitudes with which they are faced than the facts themselves. There are hundreds of examples of accomplishments that will fascinate children and inspire them to channel their teen-age 'steam' into constructive outlets.

"Who dies of bubonic plague anymore? Or smallpox? Or polio? Isn't that encouraging? Tell them about those things and the fields still to be conquered in medicine, in engineering, in geophysics, in space, in speed. Introduce a child to a microscope, to the world of creative arts, performing arts, science, to the world of books. . . . I could go on and on."

Q.: "What about sex—education and promiscuity?"
A.: "Sex can be beautiful if you make it that way. It is not an emotion in itself, it is the means of conveying the very finest emotion; it is not an end, but the means to an end. Misused, it can cause heartbreak. It could force you to abandon your education and seek work in a filling station, never expecting to go much higher, in order to assume the responsibilities of a family, right now, today. It could cause a girl to forfeit her education for the same reason. But it isn't fear of pregnancy or venereal disease and so on that causes people to hew to a line of conduct. Fear won't do it. Our prisons are filled with men who have proved that. Constructive attitudes, love, faith, understanding will do what fear cannot do—I wouldn't be here if that weren't true."

And so it went. Questions and answers until it was time to leave. The day had been full and happy and stimulating. During the long drive home, I realized I was taking away more than I had left. That seems to be par for the course now.

Last Monday night after an address to a junior chamber of commerce group, a man came up and drew me to one side.

"The young son of a friend of mine is in trouble, in jail. He has been there five days, but his family hasn't even gone to see him. He has been put in an isolation cell because he has been in so many fights. He's only 16, but he is big and strong—bright and good-looking, too. But he half killed a man in the jail the other day, hit him over the head with a wooden stool or something.

"Would you come and see him? See if you can talk to him, please!"

I met the man at his office Tuesday and we drove out to the jail. The big, friendly jailer shook his head discouragingly when I asked for the youngster by name. He said he would have to take me back to his cell, that the youth was not permitted in the visiting room.

He led me to a remote part of the jail, away from the tanks, to a grim row of stripped cells that were empty except for one. The jailer unlocked that one, but left the door closed. In that bare cell sat a tall, well-muscled young man. His mouth was a straight line of bitterness; his hazel eyes burned amber with defiance.

"Hello. My name is Bill Sands. A friend of yours told me you were here. When I was about your age I sat in a cell like this, only it wasn't in jail—it was in San Quentin prison. I was fighting mad at the whole world, just like you are. I hear you have been doing a lot of fighting. But I understand that along with all that brawn you have a pretty high I.Q. Why don't you try using it to get yourself straightened out—out of here?"

For a long moment, this youngster looked at me. Something, almost but not quite, began to break behind those hard eyes. He wavered just a little, then caught himself.

"Why the hell should I?" There was a snarl in his tough, young voice. "There's nobody gives a damn what happens to me. Nobody cares."

I opened the door and stepped inside his cell. . . .

THE BEGINNING